Krakow and Auschwitz

Vincenzo Berghella

Copyright Page

Copyright year: 2017

Copyright notice: by Vincenzo Berghella

ISBN No: 978-0-578-19070-9

From the same author:

- **Obstetric Evidence Based Guidelines.** Informa Healthcare, London, UK, and New York, USA (2007) [English]

- **Maternal Fetal Evidence Based Guidelines.** Informa Healthcare, London, UK, and New York, USA (2007) [English]

- **Laughter, the best medicine. Jokes for everyone.** (2007) [English]

- **Ridere, la migliore medicina. Barzellette per bambini.** (2007) [Italiano]

- **My favorite quotes.** (2009) [English]

- **In medio stat virtus – Citazioni d'autore.** (2009) [Italiano]

- **Quello che di voi vive in me.** (2009) [Italiano]

- **Dall'altra parte dell'oceano.** (2010) [Italiano] (Translated in: **On the other side of the ocean.** (2013) [English])

- **Preterm Birth: Prevention and Management.** Wiley-Blackwell. Oxford, United Kingdom. (2010) [English]

- **From father to son.** (2010) [English]

- **Sollazzi.** (2010) [Italiano]

- **The land of religions.** (2011) [English] (Translated in: **La terra delle religioni.** (2013) [Italiano])

- **Giramondo.** (2011) [Italiano]

- **Obstetric Evidence Based Guidelines.** Informa Healthcare, London, UK, and New York, USA (2012; Second Edition) [English]

- **Maternal Fetal Evidence Based Guidelines.** Informa Healthcare, London, UK, and New York, USA (2012; Second Edition) [English]

- **Trip to London.** (2012) [English]

- **Il primo amore non si scorda mai.** (2012) [Italiano]

- **Maldives.** (2013) [English]

- **Russia.** (2013) [English]

- **Happiness: the scientific path to achieving wellbeing.** (2014) [English] (Translated in **Felicita': il percorso scientifico per raggiungere il benessere** [Italian])

- **New Zealand: 100% pure.** (2014) [English]

- **Me dentro: i primi scritti dai 17 ai 20 anni** (2015) [Italiano]

- **Me dentro: alla ricerca dell'amore** (2015) [Italiano]

- **US Rowing Youth Nationals** (2015) [English]

- **Polynesia** (2016) [English]

- **Obstetrics: Normal and Problem Pregnancies** (Gabbe, Niebyl, Simpson, Landon, Galan, Janiaus, Driscoll, Berghella, Grobman). Elsevier, Philadelphia, USA (2016; Seventh Edition) [English]

- **Obstetric Evidence Based Guidelines.** CRC Press, London, UK, and New York, USA (2017; Third Edition) [English]

- **Maternal Fetal Evidence Based Guidelines.** CRC Press, London, UK, and New York, USA (2017; Third Edition) [English]

- **Operative Obstetrics.** (Apuzzio, Vintzileos, Berghella, Alvarez-Perez) CRC Press, London, UK, and New York, USA (2017; Fourth Edition) [English]

Preparations

I'm lucky. I get invited to talk at international conferences throughout the world. In fact, I get so many requests that most of the time I have to decline them. But I do try to accept the most interesting ones, both from a scientific point of view, and from a geographic point of view.

In 2014 I had received an email from a Dr. Monika Mazanek-Moscicka, who had invited me to a conference in Krakow, Poland. Here is a place where I've never been before. As it happens often, I had had to decline the invitation for 2015. But when she kindly offered me plenty of time and gave me a two year early invitation for the 2016 conference, I could not decline anymore. My agenda so far in advance was open, and I was truly interested in visiting Poland. In particular Krakow. I was booked for November 18-20, 2016.

This fall of 2016 I've been fairly busy, as usual. In fact, from July to December, I end up going just to Italy five times, three of which for conferences, in between the usual summer and Christmas breaks. They are all great trips. I also travel for lectures and meetings to Sonoma, near San Francisco in California, and to Chicago. I must admit I like traveling about once a month. The meetings are usually interesting, and I always learn something new. The receptions they have for me are spectacular. Just as an example, in one of the Italy trips I gave the Plenary lecture at the Italian National Ob-Gyn Annual Meeting in Rome, and spoke right after the Italian Secretary of Health. What an honor!

At another conference, on Global Health for Mother and Infant, in Florence, the President of Italy came to greet us, as the World Health Organization Assistant Director-General for Family, Women's and Children's Health, and the President of the International Federation of Obstetricians and Gynecologists (FIGO) were also attending.

The lecture I'm invited to give in Poland is on a Saturday morning, at 10:10am. Dr Monika Mazanek-Moscicka (I'll call her just Monika from now on) gives me the ok to make the airline booking, and that they'll refund me later, together with the other reimbursements and a small honorarium, which is never the reason for my travels, and I seldom get offered.

As per my usual planning I end up making airfare reservations a couple of months before the trip. I find a plane leaving Philadelphia on Thursday at 5:50pm, with a short (too short?) lay-over in Frankfurt, getting to Krakow in Poland at around 10:30am on Friday. This is perfect, as the main weekly meeting at my work at Thomas Jefferson University is on Thursday morning, and I hate to miss it.

My return flight is a bit more complicated to decide on. Given my busy fall, I resolve to come back on Sunday, so to be at work again on Monday. The best choice is to take a plane back from Krakow to Frankfurt at 6:35am, with a longer 4-hour lay-over there, before the transatlantic flight getting in Philadelphia at 4:30pm, with plenty of time to unpack and have dinner with family.

As I travel so much, I do not have much opportunity to make any other preparations for this trip to Poland. I usually read a book or more about the country, get a travel guide, watch a movie or two about the place I'm visiting, to inform myself about what to do, and about the history of the nation.

But as I'm only staying two days, in fact less than 48 hours in Krakow, and I'm going by myself, I do not have the might this time to get too excited too early in advance. But, as I get closer, I start at least answering requests from Poland to send in my slides.

Closer to the departure date, Monika and her staff ask me what I'd like to do during my time in Poland. Well, given the choice, I tell them I'd like to tour around if possible. As we exchange emails on the details, I realize I'm one of only two people invited from outside Poland. The whole conference is in Polish, and I gather they might feel awkward about having me around the whole time.

So I jump at the opportunity. Monika inserts two tours in my schedule. One on Friday around 3pm, after I arrive. And one on

Saturday around 2pm, after my lecture and session. I'm delighted. It looks like I'll have a guide. I remember how much fun I had on prior trips, sight-seeing just me and the guide, like for example in Russia. I begin to salivate at the opportunity to learn so much about Krakow and Poland.

At the last ballroom dance lesson Paola and I have with Nodari, our Ukrainian teacher, as he learns we won't make the Friday party because of my trip, he shows us for a few minutes polka dance moves, and we practice for a bit. It's fun! Too bad I won't have an opportunity to dance in Poland.

A day before the trip, my mind starts to realize I'm really going. I double check the plane arrangements. I confirm someone is picking me up at the airport, as arranged by Monika's staff. I review briefly the slides of my talk, on how to do a cesarean delivery based on the best scientific evidence.

I realize, this late, that Auschwitz is right there near Krakow. I send a last minute email to Monika, as we are finalizing the last details, asking if I can visit that most famous of Nazi concentration camps. She says that it takes at least two to three days just to visit Krakow, and a whole day to visit Auschwitz, so that it would be very tight. I beg a bit. She says she'll alert the guide, and we can decide when I arrive. I assume she wants to see if I even get there on time. My hyper-programming self needs to take a breather and be patient.

As I pack, I realize I do not know what kind of electrical plug system they use in Poland. The internet, as usual, comes to the rescue. Once I realize the correct one, one I do not think I'm very familiar with, I search my drawer dedicated to converters (yes, I have one, I travel that much), and find, after a bit of looking and studying, the right one. I'm all set now. I put my two passports, US and Italian, in the bag, and I'm pretty much all set.

Thursday November 17

As usual, after a day packed with clinical, educational and research joy, I leave directly from my office. I have walked at 6:30am with my faithful red carry-on bag from home to work, where on Thursdays my first meeting is at 7am. I do almost a full day of work, and around 3pm I book a UberX car to the airport. The driver as usual is super nice.

He drops me at the Philadelphia International terminal, Terminal A. This time not for my usual American Airline flight to Rome. I fly Lufthansa today. The name of the company is derived from Luft (the German word for 'air'), and Hansa (a Latin term meaning 'guild' most commonly used historically in reference to the Hanseatic League). This was a commercial and defensive confederation of merchant guilds and their market towns.

Hansa dominated Baltic maritime trade (c. 1400–1800) along the coast of Northern Europe. It stretched from the Baltic to the North Sea and inland during the Late Middle Ages and early modern period (c. 15th to 19th centuries). Hanse, later spelled as Hansa, was the Middle Low German word for a convoy, and this word was applied to bands of merchants traveling between the Hanseatic cities whether by land or by sea.

Lufthansa is the largest airline in Europe. I guess the part of the world where I'm headed is still dominated somehow economically by Germany, despite it lost two World Wars so badly. This reminds me of my travels in South-East Asia, where I felt China was the dominant economic superpower.

My first flight is from Philadelphia to Frankfurt. Nobody is sitting next to me. I watch first 'The making of Ibra,' an interesting documentary about the career of Zlatan Ibrahimovic, the famed European footballer. During this show, I enjoy dinner. In fact, I say enjoy on purpose, as the food it's better than usual airline food. They serve a tasty turkey with vegetables, nice and moist and tender and really good!

Then I also watch a movie, Quo Vado, by the Italian comedian Checco Zalone. I had watched it before, but it is so nice to watch something in Italian, and it's a good flick. I forget movies I have seen in the past quickly, so I really enjoy watching it again.

By 9:30pm, I'm pretty tired, and I prepare myself to fall asleep. It's 3:30am already in Europe, and we'll land at 7:30am or so local time. So if I want to sleep at all, the time is now. I have a head rest which I have inflated. Then I also have a tight wool hat to keep my cranium warm. And a sleep mask to cover my eyes. I look like a stooge, but I'm comfortable, and cozy.

I sleep for about two and an half hours. A challenging sleep, full of movements to try to achieve an impossible to find comfy position, as good as one can have on a plane in economy class. I stretch my lanky 6 feet 2.5 inch frame as much as feasible in the two seats, making sure my feet do no stick out in the hallway, where stewardesses could kick them and wake me up.

At 6am, they wake us up for breakfast. I wish they didn't... It's still pitch dark outside. After I devour the food, I put back hat and eye-cover, and try to get a few more z's.

Friday November 18

We land safely in Frankfurt. The name derives from the fact that over 2,000 years ago Frankfurt was funded by the German tribe of the *Franks*, in the place (*Furt*, cf. English 'ford', for crossing) where the river Main (Frankfurt am Main is the official name) was shallow enough to be crossed on foot. I love etymology.

It's amazing how flying now it's easy for me. I used to be so afraid of flying. Now I do not even think about it anymore. I actually enjoy it. We are about 15 minutes early, and I'm delighted, as the next flight it's at 8:55am, and with a 7:35am scheduled arrival I had a close connection.

Surprisingly, from the plane we have to hop on a bus to get to the gate area. This worries me just a little bit since it delays my getting to the next gate. And I also do not know how long customs will take. But the bus ride is only about 7-8 minutes. And customs is quick: the line is only a couple of minutes; and I just have to put the passport in an automated machine which reads it (my Italian passport this time, so I do the shorter European line) in a couple of seconds, and automatically opens the gate and allows me through after having taken a quick photograph.

While I had studied before starting the trip that my next plane was leaving from terminal 1, the same terminal where I landed, this terminal reveals itself to be humongous. I have to walk for what seems like at least a couple of kilometers, over a mile, to eventually get, after several long tapis roulants and a couple of elevators, to gate B6, where the flight for Krakow will take off from.

I make the connection without any other issues. About 30 minutes before take-off, I notice that the gate has been changed to B8, so I move a bit. I'm tired but not so bad. I do not drink coffee as I want to rest on the next plane, too. I check my email, and the news.

The plane from Frankfurt to Krakow is modern, confortable. I try to sleep just a bit more, but the flight is only about one hour and fifteen minutes, so there is really not too much time to snooze, between take-off, a nice pastry, then juice, then the landing.

We arrive a bit early. Again, German efficiency. There is very little to wait in the Krakow airport, no customs to go through. No lines. I'm quickly out, and spot at Arrivals the sign with 'Vincenzo Berghella' in capitals written on it. The driver is about 30 years old, friendly, courteous, efficient. The black Mercedes minivan is comfortable, elegant, modern, and makes me almost feel important for a moment.

Having landed at around 10:30am, we get before 11am to the Qhotel in Krakow. The ride is nice, now it's light outside finally, and I can sightsee a bit. The traffic is not bad. I read the green Polish signs, which on our way often say 'Krakow Centrum.'

Our road as we get closer to Krakow is between a river and a hill. The river on the right I'll find out is the famed Vistula River, the largest river in Poland, which goes, strangely enough for me, from south to north, through Warsaw and eventually to the Baltic Sea. The hill on the left has on it a huge chateau-like structure, which I'll find out from my driver is a medieval noble castle eventually donated to the church, and now a monastery.

Once inside the modern hotel, I quickly obtain the magnetic card for room 607, which I find out is on the top floor, and immediately try to connect with Monika. I want to go to Auschwitz so bad. I got here on time, kind of early. I send her a text message, but no answer. I call her, but no answer. I even send her an email.

By the time I'm in my room, two minutes later, she calls back, saying she is sending someone right away to pick me up. I shower and shave and put on fresh clothes really quickly. I even put my blue jacket on to look presentable, but no tie, to make sure they see I want to go on a tour and not attend the conference all day yet. That was the plan anyway.

An elegant tall skinny guy is waiting for me at the reception. He wants my lecture slides first and foremost, as he must have been instructed. I'm happy to go back up the elevator to my room to get my pendrive, so I can also get the reassurance of having my slides set and ready in their system for tomorrow.

The conference center is just across the street from the hotel. It's a massive, modern place, all glass and steel, with nothing to envy compared to some of the best conference centers around the world I've ever been to. In the US it would be one of the most modern and elegant. On its front, I read in capital letters 'Centrum Kongresowe Ice Krakow.'

I meet Monika on the first floor, one floor up from the street level, in a large room where the speaker support staff sits, but where there is also a long table for about 20 people, and lots of food on another long table along one of the walls. I'll soon realize food is out here all day long, and continuously refreshed. My kind of place, unlimited food at disposal.

Monika is super-nice, kind, accommodating. She has a soft smile, gentle manners, and caring light brown eyes. She treats me during the whole stay in Poland like a king. She gets right away that I'm ready for touring, and that, despite her saying it might just be too much, I want to go to Auschwitz.

She has actually already bought tickets for entrance to the concentration camp at 2:20pm, the earliest available on this Friday. She is afraid that with traffic we might get there late, and that as it closes at 4:30pm, there might not be enough time to see everything. But she perceives right away my gentle persistence. She pretty much immediately, as first order of business, calls the tour guide and the driver to arrange my visit to Auschwitz. We doubt I'll have enough time to see Birkenau, which is the sister camp, much bigger than Auschwitz.

She then introduces me to the handful of other professors in the room. I meet the current President of the Polish Ob-Gyn Society, Professor Miroslaw Wielgos, of Warszawski Uniwersytet Medyczny. He is very pleasant and friendly, from Warsaw.   I meet also Professor Tomasz Paszkowki from Lublin, a place I had not heard about before, but apparently the university where quite a few of the speakers are from. Tomasz has clear beautiful blue eyes, which sparkle with intelligence. His English is near perfect. He is very friendly, and he hints at a big surprise for me at the conference tomorrow. He is speaking right before me, he says.

And I meet others, all fairly fluent in English, as most if not all had spent six months to three years as young ob-gyns in the United States and/or in the United Kingdom.

Monika also takes care of business, having me sign the contract with my bank details for the refund. I've no idea what I'm signing, but I trust her completely. She has been so nice throughout this whole process, and is even nicer in person. Monika also allows me to pick in the huge auditorium, where sessions are ongoing. She is monitoring everything. While she is a bit tense, as expected, she also seems to be pleased by the large attendance, almost 1,800 people, and by how things are going.

I eat a bit of food. Most it's not recognizable to me, except some nice smoked salmon, which I eat abundantly. There are many Polish cold meatloaves, made in all kind of ways, with finely grinded meat, or fish, or vegetables. My favorite cuts are those with spinach in the middle and finely moussed salmon on the circumference.

I also have plenty of sweets. They are all good – of course I try them all!! The portions are tiny anyway, but delicious. Glucose feeds my sleepiness. Actually before eating anything, the kind waiter, impeccably dressed in black and white, has served me a double expresso. I do not drink coffee usually, as my friends and family know, but it is my not-so-secret weapon against jet lag tiredness and headaches.

At around 12:30pm, much earlier than previously planned, Monika tells me the guide and driver are ready, and I should begin to go. Guided by my tall thin blue-jacketed friend the computer guy, we descend back to the main entrance of the massive conference center, where I meet the tour guide. I ask her just for two minutes of time for me to go back up the hotel room to get rid of my blue jacket, and put on a sweater and the rain coat, the only coat I brought.

Back down, the licensed Krakow tour guide, Eliza Mrozinska, walks me a few feet to the large twelve seat black new Mercedes minivan awaiting just the two of us, with the driver in his seat ready to take us. It's before 1pm, and I hope to get to Auschwitz in plenty of time for a nice tour.

Eliza is the person I will spend by far most of my time in Poland with. She is about 5"4', 41 years old, no kids, I do not if married - she never mentions it, I never asks, and as most Poles, to my surprise, she does not have a wedding band. Eliza will talk, to my delight, constantly, for hours on end, over the next two days.

We are so lucky. It's a beautiful day, in fact it's even sunny now, and it's 8 degrees Celsius, about 46 degrees Fahrenheit. Comfortable, pleasant, magnificent! The hour and about fifteen minutes van ride from the conference center, in downtown Krakow, to Auschwitz goes by in a flash. Probably because I'm in flow, listening to Eliza pour lots of information about Poland, Krakow, and Auschwitz and Birkenau.

The modern Republic of Poland is a country in Central Europe, situated between the Baltic Sea to the north and two mountain ranges, the Sudetes and Carpathian Mountains, to the south. It's now bordered by Germany to the west; the Czech Republic and Slovakia to the south; Ukraine and Belarus to the east; and the Baltic Sea, Kaliningrad Oblast (a Russian exclave) and Lithuania to the north.

The total area of Poland is 312,679 square kilometers (120,726 square miles), making it the 70th largest country in the world and the 9th largest in Europe, just a big larger than Italy (72nd). If you are wondering, Russia is the largest country in the world, with the USA 4th, after Canada and China.

With a population of over 38.5 million people, Poland is the 34th most populous country in the world, the 8th most populous country in Europe and the 6th most populous member of the European Union, as well as the most populous post-Communist member of the European Union. Poland's capital and largest city is Warsaw, with Krakow the second largest, and previous capital.

The establishment of a Polish state can be traced back to 966, when Mieszko I, ruler of a territory roughly coextensive with that of present-day Poland, converted to Christianity. The Kingdom of Poland was founded in 1025, and in 1569 it cemented a longstanding political association with the Grand Duchy of Lithuania by signing the Union of Lublin. This union formed the Polish–Lithuanian Commonwealth, one of the largest and most populous countries of 16th and 17th century Europe. This was certainly the golden age for Poland, as Eliza says. As I'll realize over the next 36 hours, the Middle Ages up to the 18th century were the period in history when Poland was strongest as a nation.

The golden years of the Polish Kingdom ceased to exist circa 1772–1795, when its territory was partitioned among Prussia, the Russian Empire, and Austria. Everywhere in Poland, and at every conversation, one can almost palpate its history of continuous invasions, different rulers, and influences. Poland regained its independence (as the Second Polish Republic) at the end of World War I, in 1918.

In September 1939, World War II started with the invasion of Poland by Nazi Germany. Of all the aggressions Poland suffered, the six years of Nazi rule left the most scars in these lands. More than six million Polish citizens died. The shameful memories of violence, misery and death in the ghettos and concentrations camps are alive in Polish souls today, I'll soon realize.

After World War II, the borders of Poland were shifted westwards according to the Potsdam Conference. Eliza explains that so many Poles were left outside of the country. Many migrated back into the new borders. But many others did not, by choice or often by force, dividing thousands of families across new unnatural borders.

After the war, with the backing of the Soviet Union, a Communist puppet government was formed, and after a forged referendum in 1946, these new Communists took control of the country, turning Poland into a satellite state of the Soviet Union, named the People's Republic of Poland. I will learn from Eliza how everything was nationalized, and all people lost their properties to the state.

During the Revolution of 1989, Poland's Communist government was overthrown and Poland adopted a new constitution establishing itself as a democracy. Much of this is attributed by Eliza and other Polish people I'll talk to in these two days to Ronald Regan, Pope John Paul II, and Lech Walesa (which is pronounced in a completely different way in Polish, by the way).

I could tell from the highways, the streets, the hotel, the conference center, and everything around me, that Poland is now a primarily market-based economy, with achieved a 'very high' ranking on the Human Development Index, high-income economy (the 8th largest in Europe), a high quality of life and a very high standard of living.

Since the Revolution, Poland has had four Presidents: Lech Walesa (1990-1995), Aleksander Kwasniewski (1995-2005), Bronislaw Komorowski (2010-2015), and now Andrzej Duda, since 2015. His party and opinions are viewed as somewhat on the right side of the political spectrum by Eliza and some of the physicians I discuss politics with during this trip.

To my surprise, I also discover that Poland is visited by nearly 16 million tourists every year, which makes it one of the most visited countries in the world. According to the Global Peace Index for 2014, Poland is one of the safest countries in the world to live in. People indeed appear relaxed, and I see very little police around during my stay.

My wonderful guide Eliza continues to talk about the history of Poland, its economics, politics, as well as her life, and any main sites along the route, without taking a breath. I eat it all up. A king and his personal teacher. This is certainly an optimal way to travel for me.

Eliza announces we are now almost in Auschwitz. She points to some train tracks to our left, and says these are the ones who used to take Jews and others to the concentration camp. As we get closer, the front entrance of Auschwitz, a brown building with behind it a huge land with some barracks, and all around this a tall electric fence, comes into view.

I take a few photos. It's actually sunny with a mostly clear sky. I had been with Paola to another concentration camp before, in Germany near Berlin, the Sachsenhausen concentration camp. But I know Auschwitz is the worst of all the camps for fame and number of people who died. The name Auschwitz itself makes me tremble in fear.

Why did 'Auschwitz' ever come in existence? On July 31, 1941, Hermann Göring gave written authorization to Heydrich, Chief of the Reich Main Security Office (RSHA), to prepare and submit a plan for Die Endlösung der Judenfrage (the Final Solution of the Jewish question) in territories under German control and to coordinate the participation of all involved government organizations.

The resulting Generalplan Ost (General Plan for the East) called for deporting the population of occupied Eastern Europe and the Soviet Union to Siberia, for use as slave labor or to be murdered. In addition to eliminating Jews, the Nazis also planned to reduce the population of the conquered territories by 30 million people through starvation in an action called the Hunger Plan. Food supplies would be diverted to the German army and German civilians. Cities would be razed and the land allowed to return to forest or resettled by German colonists.

Plans for the total eradication of the Jewish population of Europe - eleven million people - were formalized at the Wannsee Conference on January 20, 1942. Some would be worked to death and the rest would be killed. Initially the victims were killed with gas vans or by Einsatzgruppen firing squads, but these methods proved impracticable for an operation of this scale. Therefore, by 1942, killing centers at Auschwitz, Sobibor, Treblinka, and other Nazi extermination camps replaced Einsatzgruppen as the primary method of mass killing.

Auschwitz concentration camp was known with its German name, Konzentrationslager Auschwitz, and so also as KZ Auschwitz. It was really not just one camp, but instead a network of German Nazi concentration camps and extermination camps, built and operated by the Third Reich in Polish areas annexed by Nazi Germany during World War II.

It consisted of Auschwitz I (the original camp), where we just arrived, Auschwitz II–Birkenau (a combination concentration and extermination camp), Auschwitz III–Monowitz (a labor camp to staff a factory), and 45 satellite camps. As we arrive, Eliza soon shows me a map of the camps. Birkenau dwarfs Auschwitz I in size.

Eliza says that Auschwitz was originally a military center for Polish army, in the middle of a typical flat Polish countryside. The original name of this Polish town was Oswiecim, now again the Polish name of the nearby town. Germans 'germanized' Oswiecim to Auschwitz. And Brzeziny to Birkenau.

Auschwitz I was initially constructed to hold Polish political prisoners, who began to arrive in May 1940. The first extermination of prisoners took place in September 1941, and

Auschwitz II, called Birkenau, went on to become a major site of the Nazi Final Solution to the Jewish Question.

Local residents in Oswiecim were evicted, including 1,200 people who lived in shacks around the barracks. Around 300 Jewish residents of Oswiecim were brought in to lay foundations. From 1940 to 1941, 17,000 Polish and Jewish residents of the western districts of Oswiecim were expelled from places adjacent to the camp. The Germans also ordered expulsions of Poles from the nearby villages.

Interesting, and news to me, German citizens were offered tax concessions and other benefits if they would relocate to the area. By October 1943, more than 6,000 Reich Germans had arrived. The Nazis planned to build a model modern residential area for incoming Germans, including schools, playing fields, and other amenities. Some of the plans went forward, including the construction of several hundred apartments, but many were never fully implemented. Water and sewage disposal were inadequate, and water-borne illnesses were commonplace.

The first prisoners (30 German criminal prisoners from the Sachsenhausen concentration camp) arrived in Auschwitz in May 1940, intended to act as functionaries within the prison system. The inmate population grew quickly as the camp absorbed Poland's intelligentsia and dissidents, including the Polish underground resistance.

By March 1941, 10,900 were imprisoned here, most of them Poles. By the end of 1940, the SS (the German Schutzstaffel – literally 'Protection Squadron') had confiscated land in the surrounding area to create a 40-square-kilometre (15 square miles) 'zone of interest' surrounded by a double ring of electrified barbed wire fences and watchtowers.

We get in Auschwitz I through the famous entrance with the sign: 'Arbeit macht frei,' which in German means 'Work brings freedom.' This sign was apparently first displayed by Nazi officer Rudolf Hoss here at Auschwitz, but later inscribed on the gates of other camps as well possibly to mislead incoming prisoners into thinking that their only way of securing their freedom was labor.

In the book 'The Kingdom of Auschwitz,' Otto Friedrich wrote that Rudolf Hoss' decision to display the motto so prominently at the Auschwitz entrance was not intended as a mockery, nor even to have intended it literally, as a false promise that those who worked to exhaustion would eventually be released, but rather as a kind of mystical declaration that self-sacrifice in the form of endless labor does in itself bring a kind of spiritual freedom.

Considering the role played by the Auschwitz prisons during the Holocaust as well as the individual prisoner's knowledge that once they entered the camp freedom was not likely to be obtained by any means other than death, the cruel comedy of the slogan becomes strikingly clear. The psychological impact it wrought on those who passed through the gates of each of the camps where it was seen was incredibly powerful. The picture I take in front of this gate is a bit haunting, as, without realizing it, I'm dressed completely in black, which is quite unusual for me.

The first barracks here in Auschwitz where each built to house 52 horses, Eliza says. They then housed at least 300 human prisoners each. After walking a bit in grey gravel and mud covered streets, Eliza and I walk into a few barracks, long rectangular red brick buildings.

The first photo I take inside is of a map depicting visually how all roads in Europe seemed then to lead to this concentration camp – similarly to how all roads were said to lead to Rome 2,000 years ago.

The second sign we look at lists in both Polish and English the incredible death toll on these concentration camps. An estimated 1.3 million people were sent to Auschwitz I, II (Birkenau, by far the largest) and III, of whom at least 1.1 million died. Around 90% of those killed were Jewish, about 1 million. Approximately 1 in 6 Jews killed in the Holocaust died in the Auschwitz camps.

Others deported to Auschwitz camps included 150,000 Poles, 23,000 Romani and Sinti, 15,000 Soviet prisoners of war, 400

Jehovah's Witnesses, and tens of thousands of others of diverse nationalities, including an unknown number of homosexuals. Many of those not killed in the gas chambers died of starvation, forced labor, infectious diseases, individual executions, and medical experiments.

The third interesting display Eliza points to me is a map, where one can appreciate indeed how small the seemingly to me now huge Auschwitz I is compared to Auschwitz II, Birkenau. Auschwitz and Birkenau are just over one mile apart. Birkenau was built to alleviate congestion at Auschwitz, and became the largest and most lethal of all Nazi concentration camps. It was built with one special purpose, to complete 'the final solution to the Jewish question.'

We see then a display of what the daily food ratio was for Auschwitz' inmates. A very small hot 'coffee' soup for breakfast – which Eliza said had no coffee. Another soup with cabbage and no meat for lunch. And a piece of moldy bread for dinner. Most prisoners saved some of the bread for the following morning. The daily intake did not exceed 700 calories.

For people who worked 11-12 hour days of manual labor, this was way insufficient. Currently recommended daily intake, without hard labor, is about 2,000 calories for a woman and about 2,500 for a man. No wonder many inmates at Auschwitz died of starvation.

The prisoners' day began at 4:30 am (an hour later in winter) with morning roll call. The weather was cold in Auschwitz at that time of day, even in summer. The prisoners were ordered to line up outdoors in rows of five and had to stay there until 07:00am, when the SS officers arrived.

Meanwhile, the guards would force the prisoners to squat for an hour with their hands above their heads or levy punishments. These included beatings or detention for infractions such as having a missing button or an improperly cleaned food bowl. The inmates were counted and re-counted.

Macabrely, even the dead had to be present at roll call, standing supported by their fellow inmates until the ordeal was over. Five to ten men were found dead in the barracks each night. After roll call, the Kommando, or work details, walked to their place of work, five abreast, wearing striped camp fatigues, no underwear, and ill-fitting wooden shoes without socks.

A prisoner's orchestra was forced to play cheerful music as the workers left the camp. Kapos were responsible for the prisoners' behavior while they worked, as was an SS escort. The working day lasted 12 hours during the summer and a little less in the winter. Much of the work took place outdoors at construction sites, gravel pits, and lumber yards. No rest periods were allowed. One prisoner was assigned to the latrines to measure the time the workers took to empty their bladders and bowels. Unimaginable cruelty.

Sunday was not a work day, but the prisoners did not rest; they were required to clean the barracks and take their weekly shower. Prisoners were allowed to write (in German) to their families on Sundays. Inmates who did not speak German would trade some of their bread to another inmate for help composing their letters. Members of the SS censored the outgoing mail.

A second mandatory roll call took place in the evening. If a prisoner was missing, the others had to remain standing in place until he was either found or the reason for his absence discovered, regardless of the weather conditions, even if it took hours. After roll call, individual and collective punishments were meted out, depending on what had happened during the day, before the prisoners were allowed to retire to their blocks for the night and receive their bread rations and water. Curfew was two or three hours later.

The types of prisoners were distinguishable by triangular pieces of cloth, called Winkel, sewn onto on their jackets below their prisoner number. Political prisoners had a red triangle, Jehovah's Witnesses had purple, criminals had green, and so on. The nationality of the inmate was indicated by a letter stitched onto the Winkel. Jews had a yellow triangle, overlaid by a second

Winkel if they also fit into a second category. Uniquely at Auschwitz, prisoners were tattooed with their prisoner number, on the chest for Soviet prisoners of war and on the left arm for civilians.

Sanitary arrangements were poor, with inadequate latrines and a lack of fresh water. In Auschwitz II-Birkenau, latrines were not installed until 1943, two years after camp construction began. The camps were infested with vermin such as disease-carrying lice, and the inmates suffered and died in epidemics of typhus and other diseases. Noma, a bacterial infection occurring among the malnourished, was a common cause of death among children in the Gypsy camp.

Eliza and I then go through corridors full of photos of the inmates taken at the time they came in. All – men and women – have their scalp shaven, and the usual prisoner-like striped uniform. But most daunting are the looks on their faces. Looks of despair, lost hope, fear, and most actually devoid of any human expression.

While there are hundreds and hundreds of these disheartening photos, Eliza says that at some point the camps got so busy, with so many prisoners coming in, that the Nazis stopped taking pictures.

We visit a few unforgettable exhibits. One of confiscated shoes. One of suitcases. One of hair. Each of these displays, protected behind glass, fills huge rooms. The hair must have belonged to thousands of people. It was apparently to be used to make clothes and blankets back in Germany. I picture in my head the poor souls who had to endure such cruel treatments.

Always led by Eliza, we walk in another barrack. This time we descend in the basement. There are signs that one cannot take photographs here. Eliza confirms the prohibition to me. I'm curious about what we are going to see.

Block 11 of Auschwitz I was the prison within the prison, where violators of the numerous rules were punished. Some prisoners were made to spend the nights in standing cells. These cells were about 1.5 m^2 (16 square feet), and held four men; they could do nothing but stand, and were forced during the day to work with the other prisoners.

Prisoners sentenced to death for attempting to escape were confined in a dark cell and given neither food nor water while being left to die. Inconceivable. I pause in front of these tiny standing cells, may be a meter by a meter square, claustrophobic even if one was by himself. I cannot conceive four humans in there, for days.

In this basement there were also 'dark cells,' which had only a very tiny window and a solid door. Prisoners placed in these cells gradually suffocated as they used up all the oxygen in the cell; sometimes the SS lit a candle in the cell to use up the oxygen more quickly. Many were subjected to hanging with their hands behind their backs for hours, even days, thus dislocating their shoulder joints.

Once back on the street floor, Eliza also explains the ritual of the admissions. Some newcomers were selected to work in the camp, as they were seemingly sturdy and healthy. Some were selected for medical experiments. Some were selected for immediate death, and taken to the 'showers.'

Others still, would be killed immediately by firing squad. We step outside the barrack where we saw all the horrors I just reviewed, and she shows me the wall where some of the inmates were executed. There are several bouquets of fresh flowers at its bottom. History is still fresh in people's minds here.

The first mass exterminations at Auschwitz took place in early September 1941, when 900 inmates were killed by being gathered in the basement of Block 11 and gassed with Zyklon B, a highly lethal cyanide-based pesticide. This building proved unsuitable for mass gassings. It is indeed not that big. So the site of the killings was moved to the crematorium at Auschwitz I (Crematorium I, which operated until July 1942).

There, more than 700 victims could be killed at once. In order to keep the victims calm, they were told they were to undergo disinfection and de-lousing. They were ordered to undress outside and then were locked in the building and gassed.

After its decommissioning as a gas chamber, the building was converted to a storage facility and later served as an air raid shelter for the SS. The gas chamber and crematorium were reconstructed after the war using the original components, which remained on site. Some 60,000 people were killed at Crematorium I.

Mass exterminations were moved to two provisional gas chambers (Bunkers 1 and 2), where the killings continued while the larger Crematoria II, III, IV, and V were under construction. Bunker 2 was temporarily reactivated from May to November 1944, when large numbers of Hungarian Jews were exterminated.

Eventually, the crematoria became just insufficient to burn and make ash of all those killed at Auschwitz. So bodies were burned in outdoor mass fires. In the summer of 1944 the capacity of the crematoria and outdoor incineration pits was an unimaginable 20,000 bodies per day.

As we continue to walk around other barracks, I notice the electric fences that surround this compound. Near them, there was always a control tower, with a Nazi in it. They wanted to avoid that inmates committed suicide by throwing themselves to the fences – where they would get a 6,000 Volts deadly jolt. If anyone got near the fences, the order the guard had was to shoot them.

We walk then to a building with a big tall chimney. This is one of the few gas chambers and cremation ovens still left standing, and not destroyed by the Nazis as they retreated when the Russians arrived. In Auschwitz I this is the only one remaining, because it was used at the end of the war by the Nazis as an air raid shelter. I get chills in my bones just imagining what happened inside these walls at the times the Zyklon B was dumped inside these gray, cold, deadly walls.

In the meanwhile, the sun is settling on the horizon, and the light has gotten dimmer, giving the mostly barren landscape through the electric fences an even more haunting look. We get back to Auschwitz I's entrance, where our trusted driver is pulling already towards us with his Mercedes minivan. We ride along the train tracks to Birkenau, the much bigger Auschwitz II.

The victories of Operation Barbarossa in the summer and fall of 1941 against Hitler's new enemy, the Soviet Union, led to dramatic changes in Nazi anti-Jewish ideology and the profile of prisoners brought to Auschwitz. A much bigger camp was needed to ease congestion at Auschwitz I. Construction on Auschwitz II-Birkenau began in October 1941.

Reichsführer-SS Heinrich Himmler, head of the Schutzstaffel (SS), intended the camp to house 50,000 prisoners of war, who would be interned as forced laborers. Plans called for the expansion of the camp first to house 150,000 and eventually as many as 200,000 inmates.

An initial contingent of 10,000 Soviet prisoners of war arrived at Auschwitz I in October 1941, but by March 1942 only 945 were still alive, and these were transferred to Birkenau, where most of them died from disease or starvation by May. By this time Hitler had decided to annihilate the Jewish people, so Birkenau was repurposed as a combination labor camp/extermination camp.

The Birkenau camp included four crematoria, a new reception building, and hundreds of other buildings. Bischoff's plans called for each barrack to have an occupancy of 550 prisoners (one-third of the space allotted in other Nazi concentration camps). He later changed this to 744 prisoners per barrack. The SS designed the barracks not so much to house people as to destroy them.

The first gas chamber at Birkenau was the 'red house' (called Bunker 1 by SS staff), a brick cottage converted into a gassing facility by tearing out the inside and bricking up the windows. It was operational by March 1942. A second brick cottage, the 'white house' or Bunker 2, was converted some weeks later. These structures were in use for mass killings until early 1943. Himmler visited the camp in person on July 17 and 18, 1942. He was given a demonstration of a mass killing using the gas chamber in Bunker 2.

In early 1943, the Nazis decided to increase greatly the gassing capacity of Birkenau. Crematorium II, which had been designed as a mortuary with morgues in the basement and ground-level incinerators, was converted into a killing factory by installing gas-tight doors, vents for the Zyklon B to be dropped into the chamber, and ventilation equipment to remove the gas thereafter. It went into operation in March 1943.

Crematorium III was built using the same design. Crematoria IV and V, designed from the start as gassing centers, were also constructed that spring. By June 1943, all four crematoria were operational. Most of the victims were killed using these four structures.

Eliza goes over how Birkenau worked, similarly to Auschwitz I. Prisoners were transported from all over German-occupied Europe by rail, arriving in daily convoys. By July 1942, the SS were conducting 'selections.' Incoming Jews were segregated; those deemed able to work were sent to the selection officer's right and admitted into the camp, and those deemed unfit for labor were sent to the selection officer's left and immediately gassed.

The group selected to die, about three-quarters of the total, included almost all children, women with small children, all the elderly, and all those who appeared on brief and superficial inspection by an SS doctor not to be completely fit.

After the selection process was complete, those too ill or too young to walk to the crematoria were transported there on trucks or killed on the spot with a bullet to the head. The belongings of the arrivals were seized by the SS and sorted in an area of the camp called 'Canada,' so called because Canada was seen as a land of plenty. Many of the SS at the camp enriched themselves by stealing the confiscated property.

Life for the minority selected to 'survive' and do slave labor was probably worse than death itself in many ways. We step into a Birkenau barrack, and I understand why. Prisoners were housed in these cold barracks, where eight hundred to a thousand people were crammed into the superimposed compartments.

I take a picture of these 'compartments.' They are less than 2 meters by less than 2 meters wooden bunks, three on top of each other. In each one, at least six if not seven or eight people were supposed to sleep. There are long rows of these bunks.

Unable to stretch out completely, prisoners slept there both lengthwise and crosswise, with one man's feet on another's head, neck, or chest. Stripped of all human dignity, they pushed and shoved and kicked each other in an effort to get a few more inches' space on which to sleep a little more comfortably. And this included lying in and on their clothes and shoes to prevent them from being stolen.

We walk into another small barrack, near the entrance. Here there are only holes, about 200 of them, right next to each other. These were the bathrooms. They were always full, as for the tens of thousands of people housed here they were insufficient. And all would have to hurry to defecate in the open right next to someone else. Inhuman.

Now Eliza and I walk outside. Birkenau is huge. One's sight almost gets lost into the horizon. Most of the camp was destroyed by retreating Nazis, but much remains to disturb us all. Electric fences. Some left over barracks. Some watch towers. Barren soil.

We walk for over a mile towards the other end of Birkenau opposite the entrance, along the train tracks which delivered hundreds of thousands of people who found death here. We get to one of the trains who transported them. This wagon was donated by a wealthy son of one of the victims back to this biggest and most deadly of all concentration camps. Eliza described how for many days people were crammed standing one attached to the other in these wagons, with no bathrooms, no food, no water, no heat.

Once here at the camp, if the prisoners survived about two weeks of slave labor, cold, and starvation, even these 'lucky' ones would get the same fate as those selected to be killed immediately. We have arrived walking to one of the crematoria. It has mostly been destroyed by bombs the Nazis exploded as they left, but there is enough left for Eliza to describe it. So she goes over in more details how the gas chambers and crematoria worked in those horrible years.

SS officers told the victims they were to take a shower and undergo delousing. The victims undressed in an outer chamber and walked into the gas chamber, which was disguised as a shower facility. Some were even issued soap and a towel.

The Zyklon B was delivered by ambulance to the crematoria by a special SS bureau known as the Hygienic Institute. The actual delivery of the gas to the victims was always handled by the SS, on the order of the supervising SS doctor. After the doors were shut, SS men dumped in the Zyklon B pellets through vents in the roof or holes in the side of the chamber. There are still many empty cans of Zyklon B all over Auschwitz I and II.

The victims were dead within 20 minutes. As I stands in one of these gas chambers, a dread feeling enters my soul. Despite the thick concrete walls, screaming and moaning from within could be heard outside. In one failed attempt to muffle the noise, two motorcycle engines were revved up to full throttle nearby, but the sound of yelling could still be heard over the engines.

Other poor prisoners called Sonderkommando, wearing gas masks, then dragged the dead bodies from the chamber. The victims' glasses, artificial limbs, jewelry, and hair were removed, and any dental work was extracted so the gold could be melted down. The corpses were burned in the nearby incinerators, and the ashes were buried, thrown in the river, or used as fertilizer.

The gas chambers worked to their fullest capacity from April to July 1944, during the massacre of Hungary's Jews. Hungary was an ally of Germany during the war, but it had resisted turning over its Jews until Germany invaded that March. A rail spur leading directly into Birkenau was completed that May to deliver the victims closer to the gas chambers.

From 14 May until early July 1944, 437,000 Hungarian Jews, half of the pre-war population, were deported to Auschwitz, at a rate of 12,000 a day for a considerable part of that period. The incoming volume was so great that the SS resorted to burning corpses in open-air pits as well as in the crematoria. The last selection took place on October 30, 1944.

People tried to escape their faith at Auschwitz camps, but it was nearly impossible. On October 7, 1944, two Sonderkommando units - again the prisoners assigned to staff the gas chambers - launched a brief, unsuccessful uprising. For the over one million who died here, only less than one in seven thousands, or 144 prisoners, are known to have escaped from Auschwitz successfully.

Eliza and I then walk back. It's darker outside, and inside me too. These stories, the numbers, are hard to conceive. But easier to believe once one visits these camps. Eliza then moves to describe how this all eventually, but too late, ended. The Allied Powers refused to believe early reports of the atrocities at the camp, and their failure to bomb the camp or its railways remains controversial.

In the course of the war, the Auschwitz camps were staffed by 7,000 members of the SS, approximately 12% of whom were later convicted of war crimes. Some, including camp commandant Rudolf Hoss, were executed.

In mid-1944, about 130,000 prisoners were present in Auschwitz when the SS started to move about half of them to other concentration camps. In November 1944, with the Soviet Red Army approaching through Poland, Himmler ordered gassing operations to cease across the Reich.

Crematoria II, III, and IV were dismantled, while Crematorium I was transformed into an air raid shelter. The Sonderkommando were ordered to remove other evidence of the killings, including the mass graves. The SS destroyed written records, and in the final week before the camp's liberation, burned or demolished many of its buildings.

Himmler ordered the evacuation of all camps in January 1945, charging camp commanders with "making sure that not a single prisoner from the concentration camps falls alive into the hands of the enemy." On January 17, 1945, 58,000 Auschwitz detainees, of whom two-thirds were Jews, were evacuated under guard, largely on foot.

Thousands of them died in the subsequent death march west towards Wodzislaw Slaski. The guards shot any prisoner who was unable to march at the imposed pace. Peter Longerich estimates that a quarter of the prisoners were thus killed. In March 1945, Himmler ordered that no more prisoners should be killed, as he hoped to use them as hostages in negotiations with the Allies.

Approximately 20,000 Auschwitz prisoners made it to Bergen-Belsen concentration camp in Germany, where they were liberated by the British in April 1945. Another column of prisoners reached Gross-Rosen concentration camp. They were later moved further west, and an unknown number died in this last journey.

When Auschwitz was liberated on January 26 and 27, 1945, by the 322nd Rifle Division of the Red Army, the soldiers found 7,500 prisoners alive and over 600 corpses. Among items found by the Soviet soldiers were 370,000 men's suits, 837,000 women's garments, and 7.7 tons (!!) of human hair.

January 27, 1945 is now commemorated as International Holocaust Remembrance Day. On 20 November, 1945 the Nuremberg trials began - the military tribunals called to prosecute Nazi war criminals closely involved in the Holocaust. In 1947, Poland founded the Auschwitz-Birkenau State Museum on the site of Auschwitz I and II, and in 1979, it was named a UNESCO World Heritage Site.

In the following decades, survivors, such as Primo Levi, Viktor Frankl, and Elie Wiesel, wrote memoirs of their experiences in Auschwitz, and the camp became a dominant symbol of the Holocaust. I have read these books, and I recommend them highly.

One cannot but wonder what led to all this. I used to think that all men are good. I've had to change my mind on that unfortunately. But I still believe that the vast, vast majority of men are good. So my biggest surprise, really, is for the many who knew, and did nothing.

While on the minivan ride back to the hotel, Eliza continues to talk. She is a wealth of great information, and clearly has a perfect demeanor for her job. She is passionate about what she does, and the sites she visits. It's pitch dark outside the van's windows. Jet lag tries to take over my brain, and a few times my eyes actually close for a couple of seconds, and I unplug from reality.

But Eliza keeps on talking. I'm not sure she can see my eyes, as it's pretty dim even inside the van. I do not want to miss a word she says. And also I do not want to disappoint her, as she is doing a marvelous job. I know with time my internal clock will soon reset and I'll feel better. We get back to the hotel around 6:30pm. I have plans for a buffet dinner back at the conference center just in front of the hotel at 7:15pm with Monika. So I refresh a bit, change shirt, and call my parents.

Earlier in the day I had called Paola. I had asked her what is quoted in '1,000 places to visit before you die' in Poland to see. One is Auschwitz – check. One is Rynek Glowny, the large square in Krakow – I plan to visit it tomorrow, check again. The last is Wawel Hill, the hill overlooking Krakow where the Royal Castle and the Cathedral both are – I also plan on visiting this tomorrow, so check again!

I get to the modern glitzy Krakow Ice Conference Center across my hotel at around 7:15pm, perfectly on time. I go to Ice lobby level 2 where a buffer dinner is supposed to be arranged. I walk around by myself for a while, and don't see Monika who I am supposed to meet.

So I have some food by myself, picking almost all choices from 3 or 4 buffet tables, in the midst of a big crowd of congress attendees. I do not know anyone, and nobody knows me, which for once in my life is not so bad actually. Tomorrow I'll lecture and it will change, so I enjoy my temporary anonymity.

Polish women look, at least to me, often tall, and robust. I do not find the ones here at the congress particularly attractive. I think of my good friend Don, who always told me about his trip to Poland and how he thought these were all beautiful women. Interestingly, all seem to have blue eyes, but statistics say actually here in the south of Poland most have dark eyes, while in the north of Poland most have light eyes.

I realize at about 7:40pm that Monika has sent me a text message saying they are having dinner right here in the Ice Conference Center. As I can't locate her, I call her, and then soon see her coming out of an hidden place, nice and quiet, where faculty are having a very civilized dinner.

I join her table, with six or seven other professors there already. I do not eat anything else, despite their insistence, as I've already stuffed myself at the buffet. I have a nice conversation with a nice older professor sitting next to me.

Polish university careers are unfortunately corrupted. A lot of sons of professors do well, despite not being deserving. The situation, a bit to my surprise, sounds very much like the immeritocracy in Italy, and not the meritocracy I've experienced myself in the US.

I learn later that Monika herself did not have the possibility of a good career in Krakow because she is a woman and has no powerful relatives. So at some point she was 'kicked out' from a university position to make space for someone else who was instead the relative of a powerful professor boss. These stories really anger me.

Saturday November 19

I have set up my iPhone for a 7:45am wake up call, but I wake up at 7:42am, and turn the alarm off. I've slept over 9 hours, this is great!! I feel refreshed and restored.

At 8:15am I'm at the conference. It's the Ginekologia i potoznictwo 2016, XIII Krajowa Konferencia Szkoleniowa, held on 18-19 listopada 2016 r., in the Centrum Kongresowe ICE Krakow, ul. Konopnickiej 17. Wow. Quite a name. The conference is all in Polish, with just me and a famous French ob-gyn invited from outside Poland.

When I get to the professor lounge, a pre-congress industry-sponsored talk has already started, and the huge auditorium, with its 2,000 seats, is filling up fast. They have theatre plays here, concerts. Eventually Monika will tell me that for my lecture there were a record 1,800 ob-gyns attending, the biggest crowd in Poland for our specialty.

The whole program is written in Polish. The official part starts at 8:30am, and my lecture is at 10:10am, just before a discussion period and the break. My lecture is called Wyklad goscinny 'Jak wykonywac ciecie cesarskie?' Wow! It's a review on how to do a cesarean delivery based on the evidence. I realize quickly 'evidence-based medicine' is a word and a concept the Polish academics love. So I'm their champion. I'm delighted here too study data, in particular from randomized controlled trials and meta-analyses of these kinds of studies, are the most read and followed medical literature.

I sit down by myself in the huge auditorium, declining for now to take a seat in the table at the podium with the other morning speakers. I have the last lecture of this session anyway, I can see much better from the audience, and I can more easily take any break I need for food, drink, bathroom, or if I'm bored.

The lectures actually are not bad at all. I enjoy them. First Prof. Anna Kwasniewska from Uniwersytet Medyczny, Lublin, talks about prevention of preterm birth, the topic I'm most known for. I'm delighted that she agrees with what I would recommend, that she says cerclage is beneficial in singletons with a prior preterm birth and a short cervix. She also warns against pessary, another possible intervention, and against fetal fibronectin, a possible predictive test, quoting our latest 2016 study. I feel bad I'll have no time to ask her questions, but relieved that the audience got accurate evidence-based advice from her.

The next lecture is by Prof. Miroslaw Wielgos, from Warsaw University. He is the President of the Polish Ob-Gyn Society I met the day before, and he gives a nice lecture on Rh isoimmunization prevention. Then Prof. Bozena Leszczynska-Gorzelak talks about hypertension in pregnancy, with slides that are way too busy, and Prof. Wieslaw Markwitz discusses vaginal delivery after cesarean. As I'm also taking about cesarean, I'm delighted he quotes some national numbers for Poland.

In 2015, Poland had about 370,000 deliveries, of which a bit more than 37% were by cesarean. Only about 10% of Polish women with a prior cesarean delivered vaginally in the next pregnancy. These percentages are not that dissimilar from those of many Western countries, including the US. Clearly, from these lectures, my impression is that Polish medicine is good. Their rates of maternal and perinatal morbidity and mortality are also apparently excellent.

The lecture just before mine is by Prof. Tomasz Paszkowski, also from Uniwersytet Medyczny, Lublin. He had kind of warned me the day before that he had a surprise for the audience and for me. He is a lovely bald professor probably about 60 years old, with a friendly smile. His bright intelligent blue eyes cross mine several times before his lecture, hinting something good is going to happen next.

His lecture is titled 'To do or not to do? – wybrane interwencje poloznicze.' He says at the beginning of the lecture he will review some of the most important recent studies in the field of Obstetrics and Gynecology.

Life is moments. Moments which take your breath away. This will reveal itself to be one of those times. Thomasz presents about twenty different studies from the medical literature. For each one, he has the title, authors, and journal with year of publication on top of the slide. And a quick summary with the message of the study at the bottom of the slide.

He goes on and on over the twenty studies, spending a minute or so on each. Some are randomized controlled studies. Some are meta-analyses of these kinds of studies. Some are cohort studies, some are editorials. As he gets to the end, he says that all these studies have two characteristics.

From the reaction from the crowd, people clearly have understood these two characteristics already. I had guessed them from the third study presented. Tomasz goes on to state the two characteristics of all these studies he just presented with much fanfare. First, all are published in 2016. Second, they all have one author in common, he says, "Our esteemed guest, Prof. Vincenzo Berghella."

The crowd all gets up and applauds. While the noise makes him hardly audible, Tomasz goes on to say that I have in fact 65 peer-reviewed publications just in the first 10 months of 2016. I am really moved. I'm not one to stop and think of accomplishments. But this one I'll never forget.

I'm in Poland, so far away from where I live. And I've made such an impact on so many people. Who take care of so many pregnancies every year. And Tomasz has presented our (it's always a team effort) studies so well. He really captured their message, their meaning. And he presented the exact clinical advice I would have given the audience too. What an honor. All hard work pays off.

I get up and applaud the crowd back, and walk across the huge podium towards Tomasz, giving him a heart-felt hug. I have a big microphone in my hand, as I do not want to just stand behind the podium during the lecture, but intend instead to walk around, Steve Jobs like, and keep people awake and hopefully glued to what I'm about to talk about.

My lecture is titled in the official program 'Wyklad goscinny Jak wykonywac ciecie cesarskie?' So basically all I could understand in the whole program is the line below this, prof. Vincenzo Berghella (Thomas Jefferson University, Filadelfia, USA). I am well versed on the topic I'm talking about, how to perform a cesarean delivery, surgical step by surgical step, according to the best scientific evidence, so I start having fun.

My first words to the audience are, "Gen dobre," or at least something that sounds similar to that. It's a sort of friendly "Hi Poland" to everyone. I hear and see many people laugh and smile. Then I switch to English, and start my show. I love lecturing, and talking to a large audience about something I feel so passionate about.

My slides are easy, simple and to the point, and describe how to do a cesarean delivery from the cutting of the skin, delivery of the baby, back to the closing of the skin. I always try to make it fun for me, and for the listeners, who seem enthralled. I often stop and ask the auditorium if they do a particular step this way or that way. They seem to be following along well. I give them a couple of new suggestions from the latest research we have done.

Monika had told me not to exceed 20 minutes. To my delight, they even have a running timer on top of the slides of every speaker. I have 46 slides, so I know I need to move quickly. Happily, I have 'delivered the baby' in the first seven or so minutes, and so I can now slow down and cover the remaining points in the second half of the cesarean with some more poise. I end with a big thank you to all, having 50 seconds to spare. Nobody else had finished ahead of time; all previous speakers I had seen had struggled with the timer and finished late. I'm proud of my performance.

I get a question right away from one of the panelist on the podium. I'm happy I generated some discussion, and that many will take home hopefully a better, safer and more effective way to do a cesarean delivery, which remains the most common major operation done in the world today.

By 11:10pm, our session is over, and we get to the deserved lunch. I pack in plenty of calories, as usual, receive abundant congratulatory feedback from the other professors, and answer a few more easy questions about cesarean and also high risk pregnancy issues.

At 13:30pm, I meet up again with my trusted guide Eliza, who is waiting for me at the hotel main hall and entrance. We'll spend the next six marvelous hours together. It has clearly rained in the morning, as outside the hotel and adjacent conference center the street pavements are wet, but it's only partially cloudy now, with the sun occasionally peeking through the clouds.

Today there is no need for the van. We are going to walk all day around Krakow. I've changed back into my jeans and comfortable warm shoes. I have a rain coat just in case, and so I'm ready for this. Eliza asks me first a few questions about how my lecture went and how often I do this around the world.

We start walking towards the Vistula river, which is just behind the Icc conference center. The Vistula, which Eliza pronounces in Polish - Wisla - with a somewhat harsh sound, is the longest and largest river in Poland, at 1,047 kilometers (651 miles) in length. It splits the country in half. Interestingly for me, it runs from south to north, ending in the Baltic Sea.

In Pescara, Italy, my original home, the river runs towards the east, into the Adriatic. Here in Philadelphia, the Delaware runs towards the south-east and the Atlantic. Most rivers in Italy and the USA, the countries where I've lived, run towards the south, east, or west. I'm not used to a river running straight towards the north.

From its west bank, we cross over the Vistula via a street called Monte Cassino. This is an Italian town famous for suffering heavy losses from bombardments during World War II. Apparently many of the dead were Polish soldiers, something I did not know before today's instruction by Eliza. This road commemorates them, with such an Italian name.

Most Gruwnwaldski is the bridge that takes us into Krakow center. We then turn left, and enter the most famous Polish historic grounds, the hill where its kings used to live, in a magnificent castle. Eliza takes off describing the history of Krakow.

A legend attributes Krakow's founding to the mythical ruler Krakus, who built it above a cave occupied by a dragon, Smok Wawelski. The first written record of the city's name dates back to 965 CE, when Krakow was a notable commercial center controlled by a Bohemian duke, Boleslaus I. The first acclaimed ruler of Poland, Mieszko I, took Krakow from the Bohemians and incorporated it into the holdings of the Piast dynasty towards the end of his reign.

In 1038, Krakow became the seat of the Polish government. Until 1596, so for almost six centuries, Krakow was the capital of a kingdom, with the 15th and 16th century known as Krakow's golden age.

By the end of the 10th century, Krakow was a leading center of trade. Brick buildings were constructed, including the Royal Wawel Castle with St. Felix and Adaukt Rotunda, Romanesque churches such as St. Adalbert's, a cathedral, and a basilica. Eliza explains that this north-eastern part is the most ancient and historic part of Krakow.

She considers Krakow made of three cities (see map in back cover): Old Krakow, Kazimierz, and Podgorze. She explains to me that Dietla, the main road that took off from the bridge we just crossed, used to be an affluent of the Vistula. It was covered and became a 'boulevard' (it's quite big) only relatively recently, in 1880. It divided Old Krakow, from Kazimierz.

In 1335, King Casimir III of Poland (Kazimierz in Polish), as we'll see one of the greatest kings in Poland (also founded the University), declared the eastern suburbs across what is now Dietla 'boulevard' to be a new city named after him, Kazimierz. The defensive walls were erected around the central section of Kazimierz in 1362. So this is according to Eliza the second city, which later in history was home to most of Krakow's Jewish's citizens.

The third city which made up back then Krakow, again according to Eliza, is Podgorze, which is the 'newer' part of town where we just came from, south of the Vistula. The Jewish Ghetto during WWII and the Schindler's factory were here, as Jewish families were forcibly moved out of Kazimierz. Eliza does not tell me, but in the next six hours we'll walk the main sites of all these three parts of Krakow.

Eliza and I begin to climb up this hill right on the Vistula, towards the original medieval settlement, where the kings, nobles and clergy lived. It makes sense that back about over a thousand years ago they chose this place. The Vistula is a great means of transportation and trade, and up this hill they could easily defend themselves.

Eliza describes the fact that over the centuries this part of town had at least three different sets of walls built to defend it. The walls we see date back mostly to the period when Krakow was dominated by the Austrians, from late 1700's for much of the 19th century until World War II. Eliza is quick to show me how the Austrian red brick walls were built on the ancient white stone Polish walls.

Eliza keeps on mixing history while she points to the majestic sites we are walking through. She explains that all the different foreign invaders of Krakow, including Swedish, Prussians, Austrians, French, Russians, and Nazis, all at one point resided in this historic citadel originally built for the Polish kings.

A different dynasty of kings of Poland took over after Casimir III the Great. In 1386, the Grand Duke Jogaila of Lithuania became also the King of Poland by marrying Queen of Poland Jadwiga, taking the name Wladyslaw II Jagiello. This started the Jagiellonian dynasty, a Polish-Lithuanian union. The foreign dominations all started after 1572, when King Sigismund II, the last of the Jagiellons, died childless.

So in the late 16th century the Polish throne passed to Henry III of France and then to other foreign-based rulers in rapid succession, causing a decline in Krakow's importance, that was worsened by pillaging during the Swedish invasion and by an outbreak of bubonic plague that left 20,000 of the city's residents dead. In 1596, Sigismund III of the Swedish House of Vasa moved the administrative capital of the Polish-Lithuanian Commonwealth from Krakow to Warsaw. Krakow's Golden Age was over.

By the mid-1790s the Polish-Lithuanian Commonwealth had twice been partitioned by its neighbors: Russia, the Habsburg Austro-Hungarian Empire, and Prussia. In 1791, the Austrian Emperor Joseph II changed the status of Kazimierz from a separate city and made it into a district of Krakow.

The richer Jewish families began to move out of Kazimierz. However, because of the injunction against travel on the Sabbath, most Jewish families stayed relatively close to the historic synagogues. In 1794, Tadeusz Kosciuszko initiated an unsuccessful insurrection in the town's Main Square which, in spite of his victorious Battle of Raclawice against a numerically superior Russian army, resulted in the third and final partition of Poland.

In 1809, Napoleon Bonaparte captured former Polish territories from Austria and made the town part of the Duchy of Warsaw. Following Napoleon's defeat, the 1815 Congress of Vienna restored the pre-war boundaries (therefore Poland back to Austrian influence) but also created the partially independent Free

City of Krakow. So the French influence on Krakow was very short, and left practically no trace that Eliza talks about.

An insurrection in 1846 failed, resulting in the city being annexed by Austria under the name the Grand Duchy of Cracow. In 1866, Austria granted a degree of autonomy to Galicia after its own defeat in the Austro-Prussian War. Politically freer Krakow became a Polish national symbol and a center of culture and art, known frequently as the 'Polish Athens.'

Russian troops besieged Krakow during the start of World War I in 1915. The Treaty of Versailles in 1919 after the end of WWI established the first sovereign Polish state in over 120 years, since before Austro-Hungarian rule.

In 1939, the Nazi invaded and quickly annexed Poland. The six years, until 1945, of Nazi rule left a huge impact on Krakow, certainly the biggest one on its citizens' hearts and minds. As Eliza and I pass under what looks like a medieval gate, she says this was actually built by the Nazis as another protection to the ancient city, which they had taken over and, as all prior foreign powers, used as headquarters.

In 1946, the Russians liberated Poland from the Nazis. And so started the long Communist period of Poland, which lasted until 1989. I'll realize later in the afternoon that Eliza grew up under this Communist rule. She hates Russia and Russians. She states, "We do not like Russians." And "They still have the plane." What? She tells me the story.

On 10 April 2010, a Polish Air Force aircraft crashed near the city of Smolensk, Russia, killing all 96 people on board. Among the victims were the then President of Poland Lech Kaczynski and his wife Maria, the former President of Poland in exile Ryszard Kaczorowski, the chief of the Polish General Staff and other senior Polish military officers, the president of the National Bank of Poland, Polish Government officials, 18 members of the Polish Parliament, senior members of the Polish clergy and relatives of victims of the Katyn massacre. The group was arriving from Warsaw to attend an event marking the 70th anniversary of the massacre, which took place not far from Smolensk.

The pilots were attempting to land at Smolensk North Airport – a former military airbase – in thick fog, with visibility reduced to about 500 meters (1,600 feet). The aircraft descended far below the normal approach path until it struck trees, rolled inverted and crashed into the ground, coming to rest in a wooded area a short distance from the runway.

Both the Russian and Polish official investigations found no technical faults with the aircraft, and concluded that the crew failed to conduct the approach in a safe manner in the difficult weather conditions. The Polish authorities found serious deficiencies in the organization and training of the Air Force unit involved, which was subsequently disbanded. Several high-ranking members of the Polish military resigned, under pressure from politicians and the media.

Various conspiracy theories about the crash have since been in circulation, and are promoted by senior political figures in

Poland, who claim the crash was a political assassination. No evidence supporting this version was found in Polish and international investigations.

Clearly this is still a much talked about event. Eliza thinks it was no accident. She does not trust Russians. And she also blames the Polish as being too naive, as there should not have been all those authorities on one plane.

We move up along the Austro-Hungarian high walls, and, turning right, we enter the walls and the ancient heart of Krakow (and Poland) medieval history. While indeed most of the architecture here is several centuries old, Eliza now tells me how about 50,000 Germans lived here during WWII, as this was their headquarter for all of Poland. That is also why Krakow was not bombed during Nazi's occupation. Krakow therefore is the only major Polish city to have remained intact during World War II.

We have finally arrived on the top of the hill, about 228 meters above sea level, where the Royal Castle and Royal Cathedral are. This is Krakow's centerpiece, and where so much of the history of Poland occurred. It is a majestic complex of several Gothic and Renaissance buildings that have always presided, from this rocky hill on the side of the Vistula river, over the town and its populace below. It was named Wawel, from the Polish word for 'ravine.' We are about to see the most visited site in Poland.

What appears now in front of us is a huge square, surrounded by the most famous buildings in Poland, protected by Poland's most ancient walls. This citadel has many clergy buildings on our left, then to follow towards the right the Cathedral and Cardinal's house, and then the King's Palace in front of us. It reminds me a bit of the Kremlin in Moscow, Russia, another place where churches and kings' residencies were right next to each other.

Eliza gives me a detailed description of the place by pointing with the tip of her umbrella to the different parts of a bronze replica of the square. Many other tourists gather to listen in to her explanations about Wawel.

Wawel consists of many buildings and fortifications; the largest and best known of these are the Royal Castle and the

Wawel Cathedral, which is the Basilica of St Stanislaw, patron of Poland, and St Waclaw. Some of Wawel's oldest stone buildings, such as the Rotunda of the Virgin Mary, can be dated to 970 AD.

Wawel is a place of great significance to the Polish people: it first became a political power center at the end of the first millennium AD. In the 9th century, it was the principal fortified castrum of the Vistulans tribe. The first historical ruler Mieszko I of Poland (c. 965–992) of the Piast dynasty and his successors, Boleslaw I the Brave (992–1025) and Mieszko II (1025–1034), chose Wawel to be one of their residences.

At the same time Wawel became one of the principal Polish centers of Christianity. The first early Romanesque buildings were erected here including a stone cathedral serving the bishopric of Krakow in the year 1000. From the reign of Casimir the Restorer (1034–1058) Wawel became the leading political and administrative center for the Polish State.

Until 1611, Wawel was the formal seat of the Polish monarchy, as Krakow was the capital of Poland from 1038 to 1569 and of the Polish–Lithuanian Commonwealth from 1569 to 1596. Therefore, the fortress-like Wawel complex which visually dominates the city was the seat of power.

During the 20th century, Wawel was the residence of the President of Poland; after the invasion of Poland at the start of World War II, Krakow became the seat of Germany's General Government, and Wawel subsequently became the residence of the Nazi Governor General Hans Frank.

The first major building we approach and then enter is Wawel Cathedral. Outside of its entrance there is a guard in a formal long dress. Eliza points to some ancient animal bones which hang high on the left side of the entrance. She says they were found on this site, as prehistoric fossils, and are now considered good luck bones. I think it's a bit strange to have superstitious items right at the entrance of a church.

Wawel Cathedral has a long history. Around 1305 to 1306, the Hermanowska Cathedral was partially destroyed by a fire; however, the coronation of King Wladyslaw I the Elbow-high, in

1320, was still able to take place within its precincts. In the same year began at the King's request construction of a third cathedral, consecrated in 1364, which represents the key elements of this basilica today.

Wawel Cathedral is dubbed 'the sanctuary of the nation.' It is indeed where most of the kings of Poland were crowned and are buried. About 34 coronations occurred in this church. Given the many kings' tombs, it has also been called the Polish pantheon. Poland had kings since the 800's-900's, but the prominent periods were from 1100's-1795, and the golden age was in the Middle Ages, around the 1400's-1500's. Many Polish saints are buried here, too.

The cathedral is trinavel in construction and surrounded by side-chapels (there are over twenty), added in later centuries. As we walk in, Eliza begins to show me the most important sites.

Wladyslaw I Lokietek was the first king to be buried in the cathedral in 1333. Wladyslaw I Lokietek is actually much better known as Wladislaw Elbow-High (1306-1333). He got this nick name because he was tall only up to someone's elbow!! Eliza makes me laugh when she tells me this interesting fact while we admire his sandstone sarcophagus.

We then look at the tomb of his son and successor, Casimir III the Great, the last King of Poland from the Piast dynasty. As the name implies, Casimir III the Great (1333-1370) was one of the greatest kings of Poland. Among the many accomplishments of this Polish king, he built Wawel castle and also founded in 1364 the University of Krakow, the second oldest university in central Europe after the Charles University in Prague.

Casimir III did not have male heirs. So the throne ultimately went to Jadwiga of Poland, only 13 years old. It was important to decide whom she would marry. She eventually became the wife of the Lithuanian duke king, named Jogaila, who then was proclaimed king of both Poland and Lithuania as Wladislaw II Jagiello.

As Jadwiga was catholic, Wladislaw also became catholic, and this caused Lithuania then to become Catholic as well. Here starts the Jagiellian dynasty, the longest dynasty of Polish kings. Jadwiga died at 25 due to postpartum hemorrhage while giving birth to her first baby. Another event in which obstetrics played a big part in history. Jadwiga was later made a saint by the catholic church; I guess what you deserve as per the Vatican if you help to convert an entire country.

Wladislaw II Jagiello remarried and two sons later became Polish kings: Wladyslav III (1434-1444) and Casimir IV (1447-1492). The cathedral where we are in contains also the tombs of Casimir III the Great and Jogaila (Wladislaw II Jagiello), but the most precious is that of Casimir IV Jagiellon, carved by Veit Stoss in 1492.

In the 17th century, Wawel became an important defensive point and was modernized and heavily fortified. The transfer of power to Warsaw at the end of the 16th century did not change the symbolic role and importance of Wawel Cathedral, which remained the place of royal ceremonial. During this period, many changes were introduced in the Cathedral – the high altar was rebuilt, the cloister was elevated and the Shrine of St Stanislaw (a marble altar and a silver coffin) and the Vasa Chapel were constructed.

While there are indeed many tombs around us, I cannot avoid noticing that high on top of the altar in front of us there is a large frame with a photo of Karol Wojtyla, better known as Pope John Paul II. During the 20th century, the cathedral became the site of Karol Wojtyla's priesthood ordination in 1946 and bishop ordination in 1958 as Krakow's auxiliary bishop.

After Wawel Cathedral, Eliza and I walk out back to the large square in Wawel, and then enter into Wawel Castle, the Royal Castle. Wawel Castle was built by King Casimir III the Great, and consists of a number of structures situated around the central courtyard, where Eliza and I are now standing.

In the 14th century Wawel Castle was rebuilt by Jogaila and Jadwiga of Poland. Their reign saw the addition of the tower called the Hen's Foot (Kurza Stopka) and the Danish Tower. The Jadwiga and Jogaila Chamber, in which the sword Szczerbiec was used in coronation ceremonies, is exhibited today and is another remnant of this period. Other structures were developed on the hill during that time as well, in order to serve as quarters for the numerous clergy, royal clerks and craftsmen.

The reign of the last member of the Jagiellonian dynasty, Sigismund I Stary (Sigismund I the Old), son of Casimir IV, was a high point in Wawel fortunes. Following another fire in 1499, from 1507 to 1536, Sigismund I Stary rebuilt the royal residence. King Sigismund had spent part of his youth at the court of his brother, King Vladislav of Hungary and Bohemia, in Buda. This court had a small band of Italian artisans pioneering the Renaissance movement, at that time little known outside of Florence. Thus inspired, Sigismund took the decision to rebuild the old castle in the Renaissance style.

Eliza is so proud to show me the magnificent three-tiered arcades of Sigismund I Stary's Renaissance courtyard within Wawel Castle, right in front of us. Work on the new avant-garde palace was initially supervised by two artisans from Italy:

Francesco from Florence and Bartolomeo Berrecci. A feature of the rebuilding were the large, light rooms which open from tiered arcades lining a courtyard.

Eliza explains to me how the whole complex was modeled upon Italian and in particular Florentine architecture. The columns in every one of the three floors are splendid, elegant, and surround the balconies, which allowed easy access to other rooms in each floor.

Apparently the first, middle floor was where the dozens of bedrooms were, including the royal chambers. And instead the top or second floor, the one with the tallest ceilings and outside columns, was where the 'party rooms,' and where official ceremony rooms, were placed.

The arcaded courtyard is considered a fine example of Renaissance art. It feels indeed like we could be in Florence. But this beautiful architecture has subtle eccentricities - hints of Polish Gothic within its form, a steeply hipped and projecting roof (necessary in a northern climate) counterbalancing the soaring effect created by the uppermost arcade being higher than those below to catch more of this Nordic sun especially in the cold winter (a feature unknown in Italy) to give the courtyard a uniquely Polish Renaissance air.

The extra height of the uppermost arcade is truly unusual as it places the piano nobile on the third floor, whereas the rules of Italian Renaissance architecture place it on the second floor; again this indicates that while the design was inspired by Italians, Polish artistic and cultural tradition was alive and well in the execution.

After another fire in 1595 when the north-east part of the castle burned down, the grandson of Sigismund I The Old, King Sigismund III Vasa, son of Sigismund's daughter Catherine Jagellion and her husband John II King of Sweden, decided to have it rebuilt with the work carried out under the direction of the architect Giovanni Trevano. The Royal castle remained the seat of Polish kings for more than 500 years until 1596, when the capital was moved to Warsaw.

Before we leave this citadel of Wawel, I admire it one last time. The sun has come out again. The small fortified city is still breathing so much history. Eliza says we can take a short break, and she buys me coffee (I will never get Polish money during the trip, no need for it, I know I'll tip her later much more than a coffee).

We sit down at the bar. I'm feeling like a king. She has also brought a couple of Polish donuts. She calls them bonbons, and describes them for a while, telling me basically these are the best sweets in the world. Indeed mine is very good. I discover the jam inside it, is made of roses. It's excellent!

On the steps down Wawel Hill, Eliza points to all the plaques on the fortified walls. These are donors who helped improve the monuments at Wawel – she is in fact more precise than this, but I forgot exactly what these names donated for.

As Eliza and I finish coming down from Wawel hill, she recounts the legend of the Wawel dragon. This Polish myth is commemorated on the lower slopes of Wawel Hill, by the river, where a modern fire-breathing metal statue of the dragon stands.

The dragon, Smok Wawelski, was a mystical beast which supposedly terrorized the local community, eating their sheep and local virgins, before (according to one version) being heroically slain by Krakus, a Polish prince, who legend relates founded the city of Krakow and built his palace above the slain dragon's lair.

We walk into the city proper, and Eliza explains to me the map and the sites we'll visit next. We walk over a cobblestone street, called Canonical Street, said to be the oldest street in Krakow. Here we soon see portraits of Karol Wojtyla everywhere. A particular large image is in front of an elegant building, commemorating where he lived from 1951-1967. The future Pope John Paul II was earlier the archbishop and then cardinal of Krakow, and led the Polish church from 1964 until his election to head the Vatican in 1978. Wojtyla seems to be, to me, by far the most famous and revered Pole ever.

Eliza then points to the Hotel Copernicus, which is just

across the street from the building where Karol Wojtyla lived as a young priest. She says this is one of the best if not the best hotel in Poland, so close to Wawel Hill, with only 29 rooms which apparently blend 16th century splendor with modern amenities.

We go by St Mary Magdalen Square, and the Collegium Iuridicum, a beautiful building fronted by several tall statues, which houses lecture halls, an assembly hall, an oratorio, and a library for lawyers, to which the building owes its name, as well as professors' apartments. We turn now into Grodzka Street.

Grodzka is a busy shopping street. Eliza says that some shops sell amber, apparently very popular in Poland. From there we turn into Franciszkanska Street, where in front of the elegant Krakow Historical Museum hangs another larger-than-life portrait of Karol Wojtyla. Franciszkanska Street takes us to a park, which surrounds all this oldest city center of Krakow we are in.

Along Golebia Street, there is a statue of Nicolaus Copernicus (1473 -1543). He was the Renaissance mathematician and astronomer who formulated a model of the universe that placed the Sun rather than the Earth at the center of the universe. The publication of his book De revolutionibus orbium coelestium (On the Revolutions of the Celestial Spheres), just before his death in 1543, was a huge event in the history of science.

Copernicus was born and died in the Kingdom of Poland. A polyglot and polymath, he studied at Jagiellonian University, as we have seen the oldest and most famous Polish university, and was also a mathematician, astronomer, physician, classics scholar, translator, governor, diplomat, and economist.

As we walk, I learn about the old walls of Krakow, about the fact that there are 5 major universities and 17 other cultural institutions in this city, with a total of 200,000 students. Clearly Krakow is what Bologna is to Italy, or Boston to the USA: a student town.

Eliza repeats again that the most famous of the universities is Jagiellonian University, founded as we said by Casimir III the Great. It's the second oldest university in Eastern Europe, founded in 1364, twelve years after Prague University. Eliza could not be more proud of this revered Polish institution. The facade of the main building is elegant, and imposing in beauty.

Along Jagiellonska Street, Eliza shows me well-designed student housing edifices. Inside one of the oldest buildings, in the area of Jagiellonian University Medical College, there is now a museum around a stylish courtyard.

We walk into Market square (Rinek Glowny in Polish). It's Europe's largest and most authentic market square. Eliza says that each of its sides is 200 meters long! It covers indeed about 4 square miles, and was laid out in the 13th century. It includes Gothic, Renaissance and Baroque buildings. It includes 20 churches! It is dominated by the 15th-century Cloth Hall, or Sukiennice in Polish.

I noticed right away the Town Hall Tower, rising against the sky 70 meters high. I say first "it's a church," but Eliza corrects me that this was the Tower for the original City Hall, which then was destroyed in the 17th century.

The huge square is lined on its perimeter by stores, some of the most famous in Krakow, and in Poland. These stores belonged mostly to Jewish merchants, but were seized by the Nazis in 1939, and in fact the square was renamed Adolf Hitler Plaza back then. Eliza explains that the Nazis encouraged Germans to move to Krakow, and gave them major incentives, such as the management of some of these stores, and apartments in the magnificent buildings surrounding the square.

Then the stores in Market Square were nationalized and became Polish State property in 1946, when the Communists took control of power. That seems like ancient history to me now, even if clearly it's not for Eliza, who grew up under the Communist regime. Now bars and cafes' look so elegant, all filled with tourists and with students from the nearby Jagiellonian University.

We walk into the busy and long hall of Cloth Market (Cloth Hall), lined on both sides by innumerable stands. Incredibly, I come out of it with no purchase, thanks probably to the fact that Eliza walks quickly and continues to keep me too enchanted with all her pouring out history.

As we come out of Cloth Hall, Eliza points to the northeast, to the uneven two towers of St Mary's Church. They are the tallest structures in the square, and dominate it from this corner. I am intrigued by the shorter one, on the right, 69 meter tall. It's onion-shaped on top, as one can see everywhere in Russian's churches. Eliza says that the helmet shape is typical of the baroque period when the church was built.

We are so fortunate, as it is sunny outside, and still light. Dark comes soon to Poland this time of year, by about 3:30pm it's already dusk, and it goes real dark after 4:30pm or so. I kid around with Eliza that, to me, it's always sunny in Poland. She says I'm a lucky guy, as usually it's rainy and cold and cloudy dark this time of year.

The tallest of the St Mary's two towers, about 81 meters, on the left, used to be the city's watchtower. We get near the church, with Eliza pointing to the floor around it, some of it made of Turkish stones, and all cracked. Eliza says the Turkish stone is not appropriate for the Polish cold winters, and should have never been used here! Some of the other parts of the floor, made with white-off Polish stone, are in much better shape. But also much more uneven, and unsafe, Eliza says, to walk on.

Eliza tells me then to wait for her on the side of St Mary's as she gets into a shop. I realize with some difficulty she is buying tickets for us to get in the church. I feel bad as I once again have no Polish money at all, and cannot contribute. I plan on giving her an ever bigger tip at the end. She tells me in the meanwhile to look up at the tallest tower, and at one window in particular. We are lucky, once again, because the top of the hour (it's five minutes before 3pm now) is coming up soon.

I'm supposed to see a trumpeter come out of this window and play music. This happens every hour, 24 hours a day. This wonderful tradition comes from the story of a heroic trumpeter who played his instrument to warn the population of a Tartar invasion. He was killed by an arrow which hit his throat mid-note. Indeed, at 3pm, I see a man showing at the high-up window, and then playing a soft, melancholic melody. All people around me are looking up, captured by the moment. For a handful of Polish firemen, this task of reenacting the trumpeter is a full-time job, Eliza reveals.

Tickets in hand, Eliza and I now walk into St Mary's Church. St Mary's is a 14th-century Gothic basilica, initially built on the site of the previous Romanesque church in the years 1221-1222. It contains perhaps Krakow's most prized possession, a wooden altarpiece carved by renowned sculptor Wit Stwosz in 1489.

The Veit Stoss (English version of name) altar at St Mary's church is the largest altar of its kind in Europe. It is 11 x 13 meters. The figures are 2.7 meters high. It was created in 1477-1489, and set up by the townspeople in Krakow. The altar is carved from oak wood for the construction, and linden wood for the sculptures.

The basis of the altar is formed by a predella with a genealogic tree of Christ and Mary. The open cabinet depicts the mystery of Mary's joy from the Annunciation to the Descent of the Holy Ghost, in the wings. But Eliza points first to the center scene, in the bottom. It depicts Mary seemingly loosing senses, as Eliza points to her hands, so devoid of muscle tone.

Eliza explains that nobody really knows what happened to Mary after Jesus died and then resurrected. The legend goes that she really wanted to join him in heaven. So she is depicted here in the center bottom part of this magnificent altar getting her wish come true, by falling asleep surrounded by the twelve apostles, who will take her to Jesus.

The scene above depicts Mary smiling next to Jesus, both in the heavens. And again directly above this scene, Mary is depicted after full Assumption and Coronation, with at her sides St Adalbert and St Stanislaus. The figures are extraordinarily carved from the wood, with for the example the beards of the apostles so finely and beautifully rendered.

The altar is opened only for a few hours during the day, and stays closed for most of the 24 hours to avoid any harm. When the wings of the cabinet are closed, there appear twelve scenes of St Mary's Suffering. I feel privileged to have witnessed such a beautiful work of art.

Next, as we walk out of St Mary's, Eliza starts telling me another legend. The two towers of St Mary's are of different height, which everyone can see. The bugle call I heard a few minutes ago is played from the taller tower – Hejnalica, while the church bell known as Polzygmunt hangs in the lower tower. There are however no architectural plans that would explain the difference in heights of the towers.

Under the reign of King Boleslaus the Modest (1243-1279) a decision was made to add two towers to the body of the church standing by the Main Square. Soon two brothers embarked on the task. When the elder realized that his tower was much shorter, he murdered his brother out of envy, and the construction stopped. One version speaks that secret forces completed the construction of the tower in the name of the murdered brother.

Whatever came to pass, the murderer was wracked with remorse. On the day of the dedication of the temple he climbed the tower. Before gathered public eyes he plunged a knife into his heart, and then he threw himself from the top of the tower. This knife, which committed both fratricide and suicide, was chained later to Cloth Hall to remind us all what jealousy and pride can lead up to.

As we walk now outside in 'center city' Krakow (Old Krakow), I realize we are in an open museum really. Krakow is beautiful. We walk along Plac Mariacki, the street behind St Mary's church, and then turn right into Florianska Street. The sun is low already, and it illuminates Eliza's eyes even more directly. They are like ice, of a beautiful clear light blue. Florianska Street is another elegant pedestrian-only street in Old Krakow. It feels like we could be in Rome or Paris. It's very European, elegant, bursting with shops and shoppers.

There are churches everywhere, sometimes several in one block. At one point, Eliza stands in the pedestrian only street we are on, and shows me how from that point the facades of six different churches nearby are visible. There are 140 churches in Krakow!

We then walk for quite a while. It's only 3:30pm, but it's getting dark already. Eliza is so nice, and gets out of her purse some cabbage donuts. Now this is something new! I am indeed a bit hungry, and one of my favorite things in life is to try new food. They are small, and indeed delicious! This is apparently a very Polish snack.

This old part of town is surrounded on its perimeter by Planty Park, and remnants of the city medieval walls. Florianska Street takes us through this segment of the park, and we exit the Old Town via a defense gate through the medieval walls. In front, there is the Barbikan Krakowski, a defense castle from the 1490's, once linked to the medieval walls, now free standing, and a museum. Eliza goes through the metal model of the structures, just outside the gate, to explain them to me.

We pass by Kopernica Street, where we see a statue of this famous Polish scientist. We walk on the outside walls of the Old City, along Starowislna Street, and then Miodowa Street. It's now much darker outside. Eliza explains to me that around here there are University clinics. As well as, of course, many convents and churches. She says Krakow is a very safe city, with pubs open until 3am.

Along Miodowa, Eliza stops by a city map along the street. We have entered the famed district of Casimir, or Kazimierz in Polish. Since its inception in the fourteenth century to the early nineteenth century, Kazimierz was an independent city, a royal city of the Crown of the Polish Kingdom, located south of Krakow Old Town and separated by a branch of the Vistula river.

As you recall Eliza had explained to me that Krakow was made of at least three cities. The newest one, on the other side of the Vistula (south side), is where my hotel and conference centers are (Podgorze). The oldest one is the Old Town we just left, at the foot of Wawel. Now we are in the second historic city, Kazimierz, again for much of history independent and separate from Krakow.

On 27 March 1335, King Casimir III of Poland declared two southern suburbs of Krakow to be a new town named after him, Kazimierz (Casimiria in Latin). Shortly thereafter, in 1340, Bawol was also added to it, making the boundaries of new city the same as the whole island.

One of the most important features of medieval Kazimierz was the Pons Regalis, the only major, permanent bridge across the Vistula for several centuries. This bridge connected Krakow via Kazimierz to the Wieliczka Salt Mine and the lucrative Hungarian trade route. The last bridge at this location (at the end of modern Stradomska Street) was dismantled in 1880 when the filling-in of the Old Vistula river bed under Mayor Mikolaj Zyblikiewicz made it obsolete.

For many centuries, Kazimierz was a place of coexistence and interpenetration of ethnic Polish and Jewish cultures, and its north-eastern part of the district was historic Jewish. Jews played an important role in the Krakow regional economy since the end of the 13th century, as they had been granted the freedom of worship, trade and travel by Boleslaw the Pious in his General Charter of Jewish Liberties issued in 1264.

Krakow was then one of the safest and most serene places for Jews to live in. The Jewish community in Krakow lived undisturbed alongside their ethnic Polish neighbors under the protective King Kazimierz III, the last king of the Piast dynasty.

In 1495 the Polish king Jan I Olbracht transferred the Jews from the ravaged Old Town to the Bawol district of Kazimierz. This part of Kazimierz soon had, as requested by Jews, its own interior walls, cutting across the western end of the older defensive walls in 1553. Due to the growth of the community and influx of Jews from Bohemia, the walls were expanded again in 1608.

The area between the walls was known as the Oppidum Judaeorum, the Jewish City, which represented only about one fifth of the geographical area of Kazimierz, but nearly half of its inhabitants. The Oppidum became the main spiritual and cultural center of Polish Jewry, hosting many of Poland's finest Jewish scholars, artists and craftsmen.

The golden age of the Oppidum came to an end in 1782, when the Austrian Emperor Joseph II disbanded the Jewish district.

In 1822, the walls were torn down, removing any physical reminder of the old borders between Jewish and ethnic Polish Kazimierz. In fact, after 1795, as Austria acquired the city of Krakow, all of Kazimierz lost its status as a separate city and became a district of Krakow.

The richer Jewish families quickly moved out of the overcrowded streets of eastern Kazimierz. Because of the injunction against travel on the Sabbath, however, most Jewish families stayed relatively close to the historic synagogues in the old Oppidum, maintaining Kazimierz's reputation as a 'Jewish district' long after the concept ceased to have any administrative meaning.

By the 1930s, Krakow had 120 officially registered synagogues and prayer houses scattered across the city and much of Jewish intellectual life had moved to new centers like Podgorze. During the Second World War, starting in 1941, the Jews of Krakow, including those in Kazimierz, were forced by the Nazis into a crowded ghetto in Podgorze, across the Vistula, on the south side of Krakow. Most of them were later killed during the liquidation of the ghetto or in death camps. Kazimierz instead became slums, according to Eliza, until 1990, the end of the Communist era.

Today Kazimierz is instead one of the major tourist attractions of Krakow and an important center of cultural life of the city. Eliza explains to me that I'm entering basically the district of Krakow similar to what Soho is to New York, Trastevere is to Rome, or Montmartre is to Paris.

As we walk into the district, I have to pee, and Eliza nonchalantly walks me into a Jewish hotel/restaurant in front of us. The place is elegant, restored to its old glory. There are several old maps of Krakow hanging from the walls, and I buy one as souvenir (see back cover). It clearly depicts how a natural branch of the Vistula surrounded this district of Kazimierz and made it an island until the late 19th century. Now I get it!

We are in the core of the old Jewish district. Krakow was home to 65,000 Jews, 25% of the entire population, before the

Nazis. Even the Communists supported Palestine, so that times remained difficult for the Jews also after WWII. Jewish were kicked out in the pogroms of the 1960's, leading to huge migration. Some Jews remained, changed their last names, and lived underground. They could not find jobs.

On Jozefa Street, Eliza points to two stars of David carved in the front of a house, to designate it as a place where Jewish people lived. In Plac Nowy, there are several natives having 'fast food' at local small shops, like in my town residents do at Pat's or Geno's in South Philadelphia, where cheese steaks reign. Here instead they are having something like a toasted roll cut in half on its long side with on top all kinds of meats and cheeses. It looks delicious, and is apparently real cheap.

Along Bozego Ciala, we go by Corpus Christy, a Catholic church. It's remarkable how for centuries different religions lived so pacifically next to each other, and how much that all changed so viciously. We must all cherish each other, always, and embrace our differences.

Having headed south-east, we are now along the left bank of the Vistula River, on its north boulevard, called Bulwar Kurlandzki. The bright lights of the city of Krakow light the dark evening, and glitter over the black waters of this ancient river.

The brightest lights here are those of a pedestrian bridge. In fact, its illumination changes, with soft pastel colors such as light yellow, or purple, or green. It's very modern, curvilinear, aerodynamic, aesthetically pleasing, and allows only pedestrians in a lane and bikes in the other. It reminds me of similar bridges in London and Rome.

Opened on September 30th, 2010, the Father Bernatek Footbridge straddles the Vistula River just south of the center, linking the districts of Kazimierz - where we are coming from - and Podgorze. The leaf-shaped, 130 meter structure has a modern twin walkway design.

As we walk over the bridge, I notice that over its railings there are thousands of padlocks. They are all different, of diverse colors, sizes, ages. These were placed here by lovers, who pledged their union by throwing away the padlock key over the bridge, staying united forever. The lovers' names or initials are engraved on the lock, as evidence of their unbreakable bond and commitment to each other. I'm a hopeless romantic, and so I am keen on this kind of stuff.

On the other side of the bridge, we are in Podgorze. This district of Krakow, situated on the right (southern) bank of the Vistula River, is at the foot of Lasota Hill.

The oldest man-made structure in Podgorze is the Krakus Mound, believed to be the grave of the legendary Prince Krakus. It is the largest prehistoric mound in Poland and one of the best view points in the city. The name Podgorze in fact can be roughly translated to 'the base of a hill.'

Initially a small settlement, in the years following the First Partition of Poland the town's development was promoted by the Austria-Hungary Emperor Joseph II who in 1784 granted it city status, as the Royal Free City of Podgorze. In the following years it was a self-governing administrative unit. After the Third Partition of Poland in 1795 and the takeover of the entire city by the Empire, Podgorze lost it political role of an independent suburb across the river from Old Krakow.

Towards the end of the Austrian rule, in 1915 the size of Podgorze reached about 20% of the size of Krakow. Since the return of Poland's independence, it remained integrated into the city. It includes the historic part of Podgorze with the triangular market square and impressive St. Joseph Church as well as the site of the Nazi Krakow Ghetto and the factory of Oskar Schindler, who saved nearly 1,200 Jews from the camps.

As Eliza and I enter Podgorze, she in fact points to the Church of St Joseph, lighted in the dark background, a massive structure, and a nice mix of gothic and byzantine architecture, jetting tall into the black sky. As we walk further along, she points to the City Council in a square. This part of town used to have 320 houses, and 17,000 people, and is where she was born and grew up.

Eliza goes on a long recount of her youth growing up in this district. This was a sad place, as it had been just before her birth a place of deportation. The Jewish Ghetto was empty in fact after 1943 since all of them had been killed by then. She is impressed I'm writing down everything she says; she says it is the first time anyone writes while she works as a guide.

Eliza grew up in Communist times, under Russian influence. She recalls there was little to no food in stores. Houses were all 'nationalized,' that is owned by the Polish government. Nobody was a house owner anymore. In fact everything was nationalized.

All around us now, in November 2016, appears dark, gloomy, desolate, even after all these years, and the end of both the Nazi and Communist regimes. But one can almost palpate the history here, and the sorrow, the depression, the tragic memories chiseled into the citizens' hearts.

Eliza shows me the spot where the house where she grew up used to be. She recalls it was small, cold, with an outside bathroom. The Communists built new houses in 1980's, so most of this quarter is not what it used to be when she grew up. But even the 'new' houses appear cold, impersonal.

Eliza recalls with some happiness the end of the Communist regime. Starting in 1990, the population could begin to claim back their old houses. This had to be done searching and looking back at documents from before the end of WWII. While some were able to reclaim what was theirs, many did not, as documents were lost, or damaged, or contradictory at times.

The government also passed a law saying that after a certain number of years, whoever had lived in the apartment would have a claim at owning it. So at times two families, that of the original owners, and that of the long-term occupant, would claim, with legal right to do so, the same residence. Hundreds of legal battles started, some of them still continuing to this day. Some involve relatives of deceased owners, who died under the Nazi regime. I can only imagine the difficulties of sorting out such intricate disputes, full of sad stories of death and injustice.

Along Lwowska Street, Eliza points to a tall wall, still sturdy and massive on the side of this road. This is a remnant of the

Jewish Ghetto wall. It's 12 meters, or about 40 feet, tall. On it, there is a commemorative plaque, in Hebrew and in Polish. It reads, "Here they lived, suffered and perished at the hands of Hitler's executioners. From here they began their final journey to the death camps." The wall encased the Jewish Ghetto from 1941 to 1943.

This Ghetto was formally established on 3 March 1941 here in the Podgorze district. Soon, 15,000 Jews were crammed into an area previously inhabited by 3,000 people who used to live in a district consisting of 30 streets, 320 residential buildings, and 3,167 rooms. As a result, one apartment was allocated to every four Jewish families, and many less fortunate lived on the street.

The Ghetto was surrounded by these newly built walls that kept it separated from the rest of the city. In a grim foreshadowing of the near future, these walls contained brick panels in the shape of tombstones. All windows and doors that opened onto the 'Aryan' side were ordered to be bricked up. Only four guarded entrances allowed traffic to pass in or out.

From 30 May 1942 onward, the Nazis began systematic deportations from the Ghetto to surrounding concentration camps. Thousands of Jews were transported in the succeeding months as part of the Aktion Krakau headed by SS-Oberführer Julian Scherner. Jews were assembled on Zgody Square first and then escorted to the railway station in Prokocim.

Zgody Square is now Plac Bohaterow Getta, or Ghetto Heroes Square in English. It's where Eliza has just taken me. It's big, dark, and haunting. As I look closer, there are about 70 tall metal chairs scattered around the whole square.

This memorial to the Jews of the Krakow Ghetto was inaugurated on December 8th, 2005. The winning project by Krakow architects Piotr Lewicki and Kazimierz Latak included 33 steel and cast iron chairs (1.4 meters high) in the square and 37 smaller chairs (1.2 meters high) standing on the edge of the square and at tram stops. Each chair is supposed to represent 1,000 killed Jews (as we said above, it was estimated that Krakow had one of the biggest Jewish population in all of Europe, about 65,000 to

75,000). The memorial's chairs intrude to bus and tram stops and are used by locals awaiting transportation, suggesting that anyone can be a victim.

The first transport from here, Ghetto Heroes Square in the center of the old Ghetto, consisted of 7,000 people; the second, of an additional 4,000 Jews deported to Belzec death camp on 5 June 1942. On 13–14 March 1943, the final 'liquidation' of the ghetto was carried out under the command of SS-Untersturmführer Amon Göth (his SS rank being the equivalent to a 2nd Lieutenant). Eight thousand Jews deemed able to work were transported to the Plaszow labor camp. Those deemed unfit for work – some 2,000 Jews – were killed in the streets of the Ghetto with the use of 'Trawniki men' police auxiliaries. Any remaining were sent to Auschwitz.

Eliza goes on to tell me other poignant stories regarding life in the Ghetto. The only pharmacy enclosed within the Krakow Ghetto boundary belonged to the Polish Roman Catholic pharmacist Tadeusz Pankiewicz, permitted by the German authorities to operate his 'Under the Eagle Pharmacy' there upon his request. It was located in one of the corners of the square.

The scarce medications and tranquillizers supplied to the Ghetto's residents often free of charge – apart from health-care considerations – contributed to their survival. Pankiewicz also passed around hair dyes to Jews compelled to cross the Ghetto walls illegally. In recognition of his heroic deeds in helping countless Jews in the Ghetto during the Holocaust, he was bestowed the title of the Righteous among the Nations by Yad Vashem on February 10th, 1983. Pankiewicz is the author of a book describing, among other events, the Ghetto liquidation.

There are many others on the list of Polish Righteous from Krakow, including Maria and Bronislaw Florek who lived at Czyzowka Street and saved Goldberger and Nichtberger families. Maria Florek smuggled forged identity papers procured at the Emalia Factory of Oskar Schindler (without his awareness), for the Jews hiding on the 'Aryan side' of Krakow.

Polish gynecologist Dr Helena Szlapak turned her home at Garbarska Street into a safe house for trafficked Jews and distribution of falsified documents as well as secret messages and storage of photographs from Auschwitz. She attended to sick Jews in hiding and placed them in hospitals under false identities.

This part of town, Podgorze, is of course also where the famed Schindler's factory is. Oskar Schindler (28 April 1908 – 9 October 1974) was a German industrialist, spy, and member of the Nazi Party who is credited with saving the lives of 1,200 Jews during the Holocaust by employing them in his enamelware and ammunitions factories.

Schindler's notoriety comes also from the 1982 novel Schindler's Ark, and the subsequent 1993 film Schindler's List, with Steven Spielberg as Director and Liam Neeson playing the protagonist. Both works reflect his life as that of an opportunist initially motivated by profit, who came to show extraordinary initiative, tenacity and dedication to save the lives of his Jewish employees.

Schindler grew up in Zwittau, Moravia, and worked in several trades until he joined the Abwehr, the intelligence service of Nazi Germany, in 1936. He enlisted in the Nazi Party in 1939. Prior to the German occupation of Czechoslovakia in 1938, he collected information on railways and troop movements for the German government. Schindler continued to collect information for the Nazis while working in Poland in 1939 before the invasion at the start of World War II.

In 1939, Schindler acquired an enamelware factory in Krakow, which employed about 1,750 workers, of whom 1,000 were Jews at the factory's peak in 1944. His Abwehr connections helped him to protect his Jewish workers from deportation and death in the Nazi concentration camps. As time went on, Schindler had to give Nazi officials ever larger bribes and gifts of luxury items obtainable only on the black market to keep his workers safe.

By July 1944, Germany was losing the war; the SS began closing down the easternmost concentration camps and deporting the remaining prisoners westward. Many were killed in Auschwitz and Gross-Rosen concentration camps. Schindler convinced SS-Hauptsturmführer Amon Göth, commandant of the nearby Krakow-Plaszow concentration camp, to allow him to move his factory to Brünnlitz in the Sudetenland, thus sparing his workers from almost certain death in the gas chambers.

Using names provided by Jewish Ghetto Police officer Marcel Goldberg, Göth's secretary Mietek Pemper compiled and typed the list of 1,200 Jews who travelled to Brünnlitz in October 1944. Schindler continued to bribe SS officials to prevent the execution of his workers until the end of World War II in Europe in May 1945, by which time he had spent his entire fortune on bribes and black-market purchases of supplies for his workers.

At 6pm, we are back to my hotel. Eliza and I have walked for over 6 hours, visited all major parts of Krakow, and relived over a millennium of amazing history. I'm full of fantastic new understanding of the history of this fascinating part of the world, where so many crucial events occurred. The $40 tip I give Eliza is super-well deserved.

After a brief stay in the room in the hotel, with calls to family, I have to get ready again for dinner. Monika, the professor who invited me here to Krakow, has organized a dinner out. I'm unaware where we are going and how many people will be coming, but, as guest of honor, feel obliged to go, even if I'm pretty tired.

The kind driver of the Mercedes van picks us up at the hotel, and Monika, me, and a ob-gyn professor from Lublin (who studied two years in Rochester, New York, and whose English is fluent – he must have been chosen on purpose) are driven to an 'Italian' restaurant, about ten minutes from the hotel. The food is good, and the company even better. The Lublin professor is very outgoing, and talks a lot. I hear a whole lot more about Poland.

I learn that 'dobra' means 'ok,' 'all is well.' It's used continuously in conversation. Apparently November 11th, 1918, is the day of Polish independence after 123 years of Austrian dominance. 'Clinic' means 'university.' The title of 'Professor' is given directly by the president, and kept forever.

Some of the stories Monika and the professor from Lublin tell me escape my full comprehension, as they are testimonies from this part of the world I've never heard before. For example, they tell me about Stepan Bandera. He was apparently a Ukrainian political activist and a leader of the nationalist and independence movement of Ukraine.

In the early months of World War II he cooperated with Nazi Germany, but when he declared a Ukrainian independent state, he was arrested in 1941 and later imprisoned in the Sachsenhausen concentration camp (the one I visited in the past, near Berlin). In 1944, with Germany rapidly losing its supremacy in the war before the advancing Allies, Bandera was released, in the hope that he would deter the advancing Soviet forces. After the war, in 1959, in Munich, Germany, Bandera was assassinated by the KGB (Soviet security agency).

On 22 January 2010, the outgoing President of Ukraine, Viktor Yushchenko, awarded Bandera the posthumous title of Hero of Ukraine. The award was condemned by the European

Parliament, Russian, Polish and Jewish organizations, and was declared illegal by the following president, Viktor Yanukovych, and in a court decision in April 2010. In January 2011, the award was officially annulled. Bandera remains a controversial figure today both in Ukraine and internationally. Even Eliza and the professor from Lublin argue over his legacy.

They talk about genocide in Ukraine in 1942, with about 200,000 killed, and subsequently 500,000 Ukrainian immigrating to Poland. They despair thinking how Warsaw, the capital of Poland, was completely destroyed during WWII.

They recount modern life in Poland. Doctors do not do well, with many earning less than Euro 1,000 per month. Even a full professor makes only about Euro 1,500 per month. By adding some private practice, earnings can be increased. The system sounds very similar to the Italian one. Pensions can be only Euro 300 per month, as the Lublin professor is decrying he will get. Despite all this, medical school costs about Euro 25,000, so many Polish students go and study abroad. Given the difficult financial situation, over two million Polish citizens have emigrated after 1989.

Monika and the Lublin ob-gyn professor then go over what seems to be an obsession of Polish people, as previously told me by Eliza. On 10 April 2010, a plane was carrying the Poland President Lech Kaczynski, his wife Maria Kaczynska, and other top Polish public and military figures from Warsaw to commemorate the Katyn massacre. The plane crashed while approaching Smolensk Air Base in Russia. 96 people were killed in the crash. My two dinner friends argue for a while about responsibilities and where the truth lies, without coming to a conclusion or an agreement.

I've been fascinated by all this history of Poland, and the sharp reactions it generates in all of us. Monika, so kindly, promises to send me the best book around on the history of Poland, by Norman Davis. It will come to my mail about a month later, to my rejoicing.

Sunday November 20

I cannot fall asleep. I wake up at 4:30am with a headache. But despite it all, happy. I've had two fantastic days in Krakow. I shower, and rejuvenate. I make sure all is empty in the room. I go down at 4:47am. I just give my room key – badge, and 30 seconds later, while outside is pitch dark, my beloved large black elegant Mercedes minivan appears, just for me. The driver is super nice, and in 25 minutes, much quicker than usual, given there is nobody on the dim roads, we are at Krakow airport.

My 40 hours in Poland have been great. I think how easy it is these days to hop around the world. It's cloudy all over this part of Europe during my flight from Krakow to Frankfurt. I do not think there is much sun over Poland or Germany during the winter months. I'm lucky I live in Philadelphia, while despite being cold in the winter, it's almost always sunny.

In Frankfurt Airport, I get to gate Z21 in about 30 minutes from the gate where I had landed, after doing a 15 minute line for passport control, and walking a bit to the gate. It's now only about 9am. I'm so lucky I have almost four hours at least until my next Lufthansa flight 426 for Philadelphia leaves. Four hours all to spend with my computer, after an expresso to keep me awake, and a chocolate donut to sweeten it all up.

I realize the plugs in Germany are the same as in Poland!! Yes!! My computer and iPhone get powered up to the maximum.

The flight back is pleasant. Once again nobody is sitting besides me. Like last time, this is not just luck: I had changed seats the day before when I checked in online, and chose a beautiful window seat, 20A, with nobody next to it. I can stretch, and soon after take-off a stuporous state overwhelms me, so that I get about 2-3 hours of deep and restoring sleep.

Later, as the batteries to my MacBook Air finally die, a friendly steward allows me to recharge it in business class. A trip to remember.

Acknowledgments

My gratitude to Paola Luzi for help with editing of this book.

.